The BMW Family Tree

1896
Fahrzeugfabrik Eisenach
(Decauvilles under licence
Eisenachs & Wartburgs)

1904
Fahrzeugfabrik Eisenach
(Dixis)

1918
Gothaer Waggonfabrik
(Dixis)

1919
Re-named Dixi-Werke
(Dixis)

1921
Shapiro Group buys
Gothaer Waggonfabrik
and with it Dixi-Werke
(Dixis)

1928 (early)
Austin Seven Licence

1928
BMW buys Dixi-Werke
from Shapiro

1911
Gustav Otto
Flugmaschinenfabrik
Munchen
(Biplanes)

1915
Otto-Werke
Gustav Otto
Munchen
(Biplanes)

1916
Bayrerische
Flugzeugwerke AG
(Biplanes)

1913
Rapp-Motoren Werke
(Aero Engines)

1917
BMW GmbH
(Planes & Engines)

1918 & 1922
Reincorporated.

1923
BMW – first Motor Cycle

1928
First BMW Dixi

1929
First BMW car

1933
First 6-Cylinder car

1945
Works Dismantled
Eisenach Factory taken over
by Russians

1951
First Post-War car

1959
Financial difficulties and
threatened take-over.
Half Aero engine subsidiary
(BMW Triebwerkbau) sold to
MAN and known henceforth as
MAN Turbo GmbH

1966
BMW buys Glas.

BMW The Bavarian Motor Works

The finest looking BMW's have always been coupés — and here are two of the best. Above is the pre-war 327/8 and below the 1976 630 CS introduced at the Geneva Show. Nearly 40 years separate these two models.

BMW

The Bavarian Motor Works

Michael Frostick

DALTON WATSON LTD

LONDON

First Published 1976

ISBN 0 901564 206

Library of Congress Catalog Card Number 75-19890

© Dalton Watson Ltd 1976

Process Engravings by Star Illustration Works Ltd
Printed in England by the Lavenham Press Ltd
for the publishers
DALTON WATSON LTD
76 Wardour Street, London W1V 4AN

Distributed in the U.S.A. by
Motorbooks International
3501 Hennepin Avenue South
Minneapolis
Minnesota 55408

Preface

As with other books in this series, there is no intention that this should be a history of the BMW company, even if it is a review of the many cars they have made. On the other hand, in this particular instance, there are matters of historical importance which need to be cleared up.

It has been usual in the past to regard the Bayerische Motoren Werke as one of the younger companies in the industry; and to regard the commencement of its motor car manufacturing as from the date on which the company bought the "Dixi-Werke" from the "Gothaer Waggonfabrik A.G." — that is to say the 14th of November 1928. This of course does not belie the company's true beginnings, on the 15th March 1911, when Gustav Otto (son of Nikolaus August Otto, creator of the "Otto-cycle" or four-stroke engine) created the "Gustav Otto Flugmaschinenfabrik Munchen" on the eastern end of Munich's Oberwiesenfeld Airport, in Lerchenaur Strasse, where the present headquarters still are.

So far so good, but one does not date the beginnings of car manufacture at Mercedes Benz from 1926 when the two firms of Daimler and Benz came together, any more than one would attempt to chronicle the British Leyland organisation without due regard to its many precursors. It seems logical therefore in this instance, to trace not only the Lerchenaur Strasse side back to its beginnings; but also to review what one might call the 'distaff side' back to the start of the Dixi company in the fortress town of Eisenach in 1898.

This gives us a run of cars, from the first Decauvilles built under licence, through a range of models usually called Wartburgs, but occasionally referred to (as by Gerald Rose in his "Record of Motor Racing") as Eisenachs, on to the very successful and sporting Dixis. Then come the first of the Austin Sevens built under licence by that firm when BMW took it over, and the name Wartburg was once more employed. One ought perhaps to make it especially clear that there is no connection at all with the present range of cars bearing the name of the Wartburg castle in Eisenach; and now behind the "Iron Curtain".

One last word must also be due in the matter of motor cycles. To write a book about BMW cars and then include bikes might seem to be flying in the face of common sense; but since the BMW company itself produced the famous two wheeler before they even considered cars, and because these machines themselves have such a record and are of such excellence, and because in one of their very dark hours the company only survived by making a car with the motor cycle engine in it — they cannot in all conscience be left out: — besides which I didn't want to.

J.M.F.

Contents

Acknowledgement

I am obviously indebted, first of all, to BMW themselves, both the parent company in Munich and the British concessionaires. In London, Raymond Playfoot has borne the brunt of innumerable enquiries and requests with inexhaustable charm and good nature. In Munich my first thanks must go to Michael Schimpke and his secretary Yvonne von Widekind who, among so many other things, did a lot of translating of the untranslatable (and often illegible) on my behalf. My thanks too, to the archivist and his staff, who had their good order turned to chaos as we rummaged through their files. My thanks also go to Horst Avenarius who rescued us from at least one tricky situation; and of course to an old friend, Dirk Strassl who had been through it all before in his Mercedes days.

The Library of the National Motor Museum proved invaluable; and my old friends Eric Bellamy and Michael Ware put themselves out as usual, to help. Michael Bowler, editor of Classic & Thoroughbred Car, and himself a great BMW enthusiast, gave freely of his time and knowledge — and his photographs; and The Autocar was also helpful with pictures.

Hr. Otto Neubauer supplied a number of pictures from his private collection, and much valuable information about the early cars; and finally when photographs of the 'One hundred miles in the hour' run at Brooklands sent in the post by W. H. Aldington failed to arrive, S. C. H. 'Sammy' Davis lifted a personal photograph from his album and saved the day.

CHAPTER ONE

Fahrzeugfabrik Eisenach

The Eisenach factory was opened in 1896 by a German industrialist by the name of Heinrich Ehrhardt with a view to making military equipment; but Ehrhardt himself was a designer of some ability — he invented a gun which recoiled on its carriage — and was interested in the then new motor cars. He started off, therefore, with some electric vehicles in 1898, which were remarkable for their transmission; which was not by the then almost universal chains but by toothed wheels and shafts with universal joints.

These early models were, however, very much "one-offs" made by an enthusiastic engineer; but before long the business man in him made him drop these developments in favour of producing the French Decauville. This was the product of a famous Locomotive firm and one with which Ehrhardt might well have had associations. A number of different models were made — all of them based on Decauville designs, up to the first four cylinder in 1902. This year also saw the production of the two "racers" entered for the Paris-Vienna race.

Like the rest of the cars these were generally called Wartburgs (after the castle in Eisenach) but were from time to time also known as Eisenachs. The two in the Paris-Vienna do not seem to have been particularly successful; and the two cars were very different, the smaller being an 8 hp "Voiturette", probably of Decauville origin, while the larger was a 15 hp model which would seem to have been created for the race and was notable for having a five speed gearbox.

Both cars were entered as Eisenachs the larger one, driven by Kircheim running as No. 212 and averaging 22.6 mph for the journey to finish 27th in its class and 53rd overall. The little Voiturette driven by Enke managed 16.3 mph, but was not listed as having any place either in class or overall.

This was indeed a promising beginning and one would have expected that Ehrhardt would have gone on; but he did not. History does not tell us the whys and wherefores; but Ehrhardt gave up his interest in the company a year later (in 1903) and although his son continued car manufacture at one of the company's other plants, still using Decauville designs and calling them Ehrhardt-Decauvilles, the original factory was taken over by a new company composed of Ehrhardt's partners. They decided that a new range of cars should be produced which were to be "the last word" in Motor Cars; and by this decision they arrived at the name "Dixi". This is the Latin for "I have spoken" and was usually used at the end of a sentence, to indicate to others that no further comment was necessary! Thus Dixi— "the last word"; but of course here it has to be the first word of a new chapter.

A Decauville built under licence at the Eisenach factory and marketed as a Wartburg. It had a 3½ hp two-cylinder four-stroke engine and was in production from 1898 to about 1904.

This picture taken in 1898 is said to represent "a test run" by current Wartburg cars in front of the castle of that name in Eisenach. It would be a fair guess that the cars were not moving when the picture was taken.

197 cars were built between 1898 and 1903 — this being number 63, with Ehrhardt's wife at "the levers".

Portrait of a satisfied owner who, in sending this picture to the works wrote, "All my companions had great pleasure from a ride in the car".

For all the success of the Decauvilles, Ehrhardt remained an engineer at heart and went on with the sporadic production of electric models. This 1901 example has a Landau body and a rather precarious driving position — beyond that not very much is known of it.

A 1902 four-cylinder Wartburg — when the firm was beginning to grow up.

CHAPTER TWO

The last word

With Ehrhardt's departure the new directors of what was still called Fahrzeugfabrik Eisenach decided to produce a full range of cars completely designed and built in their own factory. They secured the services of Willy Seck a pioneer German designer; and presented their first models at the Frankfurt Show in 1904. The cars covered a wide range and incorporated both chain and shaft drive (to a point where in some models it became almost an option) they quickly gained a reputation for being well made, and in consequence became very popular. Their export business flourished and they were sold in England as Leanders and in France as Reginas. They had one little fling in the competition world and entered the Kaiserpreis event in 1907, so the story goes, although there were no Dixis in the event (but at least two Eisenachs and an Ehrhardt). Appearances were also made in the Heckomer and Prince Henry Trials — but Dixis competition successes were some way off yet.

The end of the 1914-1918 war found the company, as many others, in a dire state; and it was taken over by the German railway manufacturers Gothaer Waggonfabrik who named their new subsidiary "Dixi-Werke, Eisenach AG. and started all over again in 1920. At this point they decided to pursue a one model policy and put all their eggs in the basket of their 1596 cc 6/24 model and in the long run did very well with it. A competition programme was set out and the cars achieved class wins at Avus in 1921 and 1922, in the latter year finishing 1-2-3 with the winning car, driven by Grebser, averaging 112.65 kph. They also went in for a number of more local events and hill climbs in which they enhanced their reputation.

By 1927 there seemed to be a market for a bigger car and the six-cylinder 13/60 was introduced and then followed some more business complications. Gothaer Waggonfabrik was taken over by the Schapiro company who already owned the Cyklon works, so that the next new Dixi model the 9/40 was identical to the Cyklon of the same type. But the Eisenach factory was still full of ideas. They produced a number of prototypes and specials, in particular a streamlined saloon built to the ideas of the airflow pioneer Paul Jaray in 1924, and later on two prototypes of 2.5 and 5.8 litres were made, both having six cylinder engines.

Then came the step that everybody knows about. In 1928 the company obtained a licence from Sir Herbert Austin to make a version of the famous Austin Seven and it was later the same year, when production was hardly more than under way, that the Shapiro company sought to sell off its Eisenach factory and the good will that went with it. And it was at this point that BMW stepped in, as they felt the time had come to enter the car market.

The single-cylinder 8 hp Dixi made between 1904 and 1906 at the Eisenach works after the departure of Ehrhardt. Designed by Willy Seck it made its debut at the Frankfurt Show. The Autocar of 8/4/05 calls it 7 hp but these differences were commonplace.

The engine of the car above. Sturdy and reliable it was the common sense factor of the design which gave the car its good reputation.

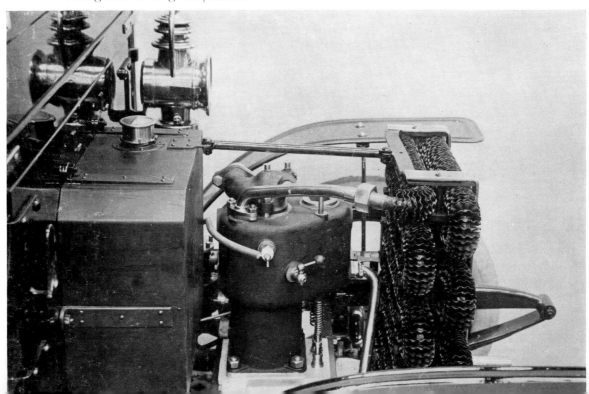

Two views of the T.24 4.9 litre four-cylinder car then rated at 24 hp. This is one of the first ten cars which were built with chain drive. Later a slightly modified version with shaft drive was offered as the T.25, of which 86 examples were built. It is evident from the cars on this spread that the manufacturers were keen on the closed car even when the top offered precious little protection.

One of the smaller cars of the same period the two-cylinder *T.14*, given as *16 hp*. *About 60 of these were made*.

Slightly grander and a little later (1904-07) the S·14 had a four-cylinder 22 hp engine of 2.8 litres of which the company made about 110 examples. Despite its taxi-like appearance it was intended for private use, for which the wheelbase was on the short side.

Two open tourers from the 1907 period. Above, the S.15 with a slightly larger engine than the car on the opposite page, being 3430 cc. In production up to 1910, 75 being made in all. Below, an unidentified model now in the Eisenach Museum. Probably the same as the "taxi" opposite and certainly a smaller car than the one above.

According to the records these are both the same car — the T.20. A four-cylinder 40 hp 4.3 litre model that was in production from 1910 to 1913 and of which about 77 were made. Close examination shows a marked similarity in body, save for the modified bonnet line, and the addition of front doors to the later model.

Made up to 1912, this is the U35/3 of which there were 56, at the very high price of 16,000 marks for the cheapest model. Below, a late version of the above car, with side mounted battery and indicator.

The small R.9 model of 1900 cc made from 1911 to 1913, there were 175 of them. There is an enchanting similarity in the coach lines of all these cars with a flourish of quite French feeling, and signs of high cost in the bevelled glass of the windows.

Below and on the opposite page two interiors of the period. Unfortunately no caption remains for the smaller car below; but the picture on the right is of the interior of the 1912 55 hp model and was used in catalogues and advertisements to demonstrate "the drawing-room feeling on the road" (note the electric light fitting).

Suddenly an ugly duckling, but one of the most successful models. 553 of these were produced between 1910 and 1920, with 30 hp, 2½ litre engines, and known as the type 12.

A real collectors piece. A car from the immediate pre-war period with a special body. Notwithstanding the special wind-cheater on the front of the radiator, and the chauffeur's goggles, the man in the boater retains his confidence.

Again just before the war with the Duke of Saxe-Coburg-Gotha as a passenger. He was a nephew of Prince Albert.

Another 1914 model described as a "camp car". Apart from the possibility of fishing tackle in the wicker baskets the description does not tell us much.

This one comes as a bit of a surprise since all we can say is that it is a "Special military body" for the 1914/18 war, for which purpose it seems needlessly luxurious — but the lovely lines on the doors have gone.

Forerunner of the family "Estate" for improbably enough this is captioned "Limousine" in the archives. At all events it is an S.16, 3378 cc, 39 hp, four-cylinder of which 710 were made between 1913 and 1924.

And here is the same S.16 with a very interesting body which demands comparison with that on page 39 of 'The Mighty Mercedes'.

This is the U.1, a 5148 cc four-cylinder of which the company made 78 and which boasts our old friend the battery box, as did the slightly earlier U.35. No one seems to be able to give the true chapter and verse of the model numbers and with the small production runs, it becomes very confused.

Both the taxi and the fashionable ladies' runabout are the same dog beneath the skin; the 1925 6/24 hp 1600 cc car. The taxi is from Berlin and both sport the Dixi mascot, a kind of Centaur with a washer-womans face and flying hair. Below, is the last development before BMW took over — only three were built and little is known of them save that one completed 350,000 kms on test!

This is known to be either the *1907* Dixi *for the* Florio Cup *(or just possibly the *1907* Kaiserpreis Protos). Comparison with the picture below makes it almost certainly a Dixi, as the latter car is known to be that, and they are almost identical. The latter, however, is said to be the "*1911 Moscow-Paris car*". No details of a Moscow-Paris race can be found for that year, so a sense of mystery remains.*

Successful Dixi's in the 1910 Prince Henry trials. Both cars carry military observers. The German Army had by that time begun to be interested in the motor car as a weapon of war.

A double victory for Dixi at the Avus circuit in 1922. The winner averaged 113.5 kph while the second car was only 1 kph slower.

A 6/24 Dixi at the Forstenrieder Park races in 1923 where it is supposed to have achieved 120 mph. The driver is unknown.

These are all virtually the same car in the process of growing up. On this page the early track cars with "streamline" bodies, produced without the aid of a wind-tunnel (something the manufacturers evidently felt keenly about: the "extractor" exhaust is also interesting. At the top of the opposite page is a road version of a similar car with large rear brakes and "mud-wings" that really fulfil that description. The last two pictures are of later cars (around 1925) when Fritz Feuerstein (bottom right) won the Solitude race. These cars are clearly road models with electric lights. They are all the 6/24 Sports car.

The *works feelings about a lack of wind tunnel were very real as they had a genuine interest in streamlined shapes. Unable to proceed themselves they commissioned, in 1924, this design from Paul Jaray on the same sports 6/24 chassis as we have seen overleaf. However you look at it this is a very advanced piece of work which might well have come out of the late thirties rather than the mid twenties — it is a pity the public response was so slow or cars might have looked better, sooner.*

CHAPTER THREE

A rose by any other name

What on earth is there left to say about the dear old "Baby" Austin? Its fame was international and its copyists almost as numerous as the more respectable firms which, on a world wide basis, took out licences to make their own version. France, America and Japan all had a stab at it; and no surprise can therefore be expressed to find the directors of Dixi-Werke after the same thing.

The cars did not appear on the German market until early in 1928, which was a long time after Sir Herbert Austin first introduced his new baby to Britain. Because of this, its image was already a little different. The ghastly cyclecars with which the post-war market was flooded had largely gone from the scene; and small, if not tiny, cars were fairly much in evidence. The Austin Seven had grown up quite a bit even in its native land though Sir Herbert never made the mistake of trying to improve it too much. Indeed, even when he got as far as the Ruby in the mid-thirties, it was still very much the mixture as before. A comparison with the Mini is direct and reasonable.

None of the overseas licences had the same sense, for they one and all started making a copy of the Austin, and almost at once tried to improve it! The directors of Dixi-Werke were no exception, save that within a few months of their obtaining the licence and starting production, they were in negotiation with the directors of BMW to sell to them the Eisenach plant, and all the trade and connections that went with it including the Austin Seven.

It is no longer quite clear why the BMW directors were interested in this deal; but the success of the motor-cycles had certainly given them the idea that the manufacture of a small car would be full of possibilities. They had no space at their existing works, so the idea of acquiring not only somewhere to make cars but some cars to make, must have been near irresistible.

So the first BMW car was born, by Eisenach out of Austin; but before you could say Jack Robinson "improvements" had set in. A glance at the French Rosengart quickly showed how the appearance could be made less spidery; but as might be supposed the new coachwork was too much for the chassis, and in the official version of their history BMW decided to "produce a new car". Not so much of it was as new as all that, but they did a good 'Beefing-up' job to make the AM4.

They also made something that looked like an Ulster Austin and called it the 'Wartburg Sport'; but Clever Dicks should beware, for not everything that looked like that was a Wartburg Sport (of which there were only 400) some of them were just plain Dixis.

Here in all its glory the "Dixi" version of the "Baby" Austin. The drop-head coupé in the upper photograph is a specialist coachbuilders job (Büschel) but carries the old type of Austin radiator suitably adorned by the full Dixi mascot. The engine, apart from left-hand drive shows several minor changes for Austin Seven enthusiasts to note; and all we can say of the car at the bottom is that it is not a Wartburg Sport. Indeed the Author has strong suspicions that it is an Austin Seven; but it comes from the Dixi archives and is just possibly an early experimental conversion.

No doubts about these — the BMW "Dixi" 3/15 with all the signs of its heritage clearly showing, and with the simpler Dixi mascot evolved for the car.

One of the first and most popular models was the so called "Sports Two-seater" with all weather equipment. The Germans it would seem were less keen on pretending to have four seats and were happier with only two. The car in the top pictures is captioned "The first BMW car" but as the lower shot shows it was but one of many. There is an interesting reversal of colour schemes the big batch having a light stripe.

On the opposite page. Probably another special; but no details are known — at least it shows that anything Mulliner could do someone else was prepared to try.

The Rosengart influence — one of the later cars from 1930 with what is described as a Limousine; but the French style has almost obliterated the original Austin.

Here are the first of the "beefed-up" AM4 models called "a new car" at the time by the company, they are none the less very much derived from the Austin. Above, the standard tourer (looking very much like things to come) and a special drop-head below with the customary heavy German hood.

More examples of the 1933 AM.4, the lower one with a fully opening roof reminiscent of todays' small Citroens — and none the worse for that. Not a very interesting car the AM.4 none the less paved the way; and was constantly in a state of development, with a lot of different ideas, especially as regards coachwork, always on the boil.

No one gets through a book like this without the mystery car cropping up. The BMW archive caption for this is simply "Kabriolett BMW AM4 3/20 PS 4-Cylinder". Nothing less like the cars on the preceeding page can be imagined; but radiator, badge and headlamps tally. For the rest it must have been lowered and lengthened, but by whom and for what is not revealed. There is a coachbuilders badge at the bottom of the scuttle, for those with leanings towards the Sherlock Holmes approach.

The Wartburg Sport. This was simply the most sporting version of the Dixi that BMW made; and for which they revived the Wartburg name which they had acquired with the purchase of the Dixi business. Like so many of the Austins it was a similar, if not identical, dog beneath the skin. This is 1928 and they made only 400 of them.

Not Wartburg Sports but earlier models with the old style Austin radiator with Dixi badges. The place is presumably the Avus circuit. Below, the victorious team in the 1929 Alpine.

CHAPTER FOUR

The small sixes

Having got themselves a factory, and something to make in it, it was clearly not going to be long before the company branched out on its own to make cars of a quality comparable with the already excellent bikes being made at Munich.

It was early in the thirties when the small six was every Europeans' idea of an ideal car. The BMW board hesitated a bit, toying briefly with a small four, and then a very small six, before settling down with the 1500 cc model 315 which is, in a popular sense at all events, the beginning of the famous range.

It is very difficult to assess those early cars accurately, in retrospect they have been credited with qualities they probably never had. It might be ungenerous to call them the German Wolseley Hornet, because history has made the latter seem less good than it really was. At all events square boxy European saloons of no great performance but with exemplary road holding, had a special place in the minds of enthusiasts; and save possibly for Lancia, BMW were pre-eminent.

They drew fairly heavily on the current German thinking, and it was the kind of mind that produced the Grand Prix cars which set about the business of making these ordinary little saloons into something quite special in the way of sports cars. The first of these was the 1.5 litre 315 which when fitted with triple carburettors developed 40 bhp; and in the 1934 Alpine Trial gained the team prize and almost world-wide recognition.

All the time the one-and-a-half litre cars were in production the company was feeling its way to bigger and better things. First they increased the engine to the obvious two litres and then, increased the car to go with it. Opinion can remain fairly sharply divided as to the appearance of the latter cars. The box may have disappeared but in its place were some well rounded saloons and cabriolets which certainly failed to develop the admirable lines of the first sporting two-seaters. But they were evidently well made and well finished, in a continental 'metal dashboard and no nonsense' kind of way and they were quiet, fast (70 was a good lick in those days) and reliable.

Then came the 327 an elegant low coupé (or convertible) with all the best of the flair which German coachbuilders could in those days muster — the bodies were in fact built out — the technical specification was up to date if not advanced with its independent front and torsion bar rear springing. Such was the charm of these cars that everyone felt they must lead to something really splendid — which of course they did; and, as it were in acknowledgement, the 328, when it came, provided an alternative and more powerful engine for its precursors.

The first of the six-cylinder cars dating from 1933, the 303 fitted with a 1173 cc engine.
Above is the standard saloon, and below one of the two-seater cabriolets which later appeared
with the larger 315 (1½ litre) engine. In all 2300 examples with the small engine were made
(including cabriolets and special bodies).

Also on the 303. The Baumuster two-seater Cabriolet. The bottom photograph has been so touched up that even the bonnet louvres may be an artists addition. The top car is at least as it was, with coachbuilders mark. All these cars show the almost day to day changes in the bonnet ventilation which ought to be a guide to date and type but seldom seem to be.

The four-cylinder 309 came into production, contrary to one's expectations, a year after the first small six and stayed in the catalogue until 1936. It was in most respects, save for the engine, a close relative of the 303; and on this page are the tourer and two shots of the standard cabriolet showing that many parts were common to both.

Two more examples of the four-cylinder car on which the bumpers were not standard (it was their cheapest model) but the pattern was set and clearly many of the cars on the ensuing pages grew naturally from these beginnings.

Cabriolets again. The catalogue drawing of the 1½ litre (above) differs considerably from the facts below. Wire wheels were an optional extra; but the headlamps on the lower car seem to be entirely individual though something like them crops up on the earliest example of the 315 sports. Perhaps the works kept them for photographic sessions.

The boxy saloon in all its glory — note the rear-hinged door. BMW hung the doors differently from model to model there was no organised progression from convenience to safety as with other manufacturers.

A special cabriolet. Were it not for the wings and wheel hubs one might want to argue that it wasn't a BMW at all (note the Chromium radiator).

Again the tourer. It seems odd that open cars without sporting pretensions should still have been so popular in the mid-thirties, they were however in demand by the services.

One of the prettiest. This two seater drop-head is, of course, a close relative of the open sports two-seater which started BMW's real rise to fame. It uses the same tail-end treatment and in order to preserve the line as much as possible the average driver's head must have been very near the roof (compare with the prototype on page 59). The cars are not all the same, the dark one on these pages (probably) a 319 as there are at this time the beginnings of organisation in the louvre decoration — but the chromium strips were too easy to add for them to be a certain identification. The light cars on the opposite page also differ the top one having the more elongated headlamps. It is probably 315 of which 20 examples were made. The white square in the spare wheel cover is the illuminated rear number plate which does away with the clumsy attachment we have become used to on the previous pages.

The 315 cabriolet in its standard form. The hood bag was a real necessity with that overhang. Below, the interior, showing the very grained leather popular in Germany at that time and also the tubular construction of the seats. These were, as are BMW seats today, rather ordinary to look at but very comfortable to sit on.

The *319* in Saloon and Sunshine Saloon versions. The latter, though much less handsome than the cabriolet, was much easier to manage; and in the authors experience could be happily used without the hood-bag. Wire wheels were also available on these cars.

The first of the immortals, the 1½ litre sports car introduced in 1934. Above, the prototype as it appeared in the motor shows of that year — with a cutaway which not only shows the layout but reminds us that only the British thought the remote control gear-lever essential. Below, is the production model. In all 230 were made between 1934 and 1937.

Handsome is as handsome does. The little two-seater looking very pretty from above (and showing its neat hood arrangements) while below the ugly duckling. It is not a hard-top, as careful study of the moulding will show; but a coupé that never got into production for obvious reasons. It should not be supposed that the absence of lights indicates that it was made to the order of Armand Esders.

Details of the sports car. Above, the independent front suspension (which was, of course, on all the cars) the transverse leaf being a very popular method before the war. In the centre, the engine, with its rather curious manifolding: but which produced 40 bhp at 4,200 rpm in its standard form. It does not have the same valve arrangement as the later 328 — this is a straightforward push-rod design. Below, the dash. White faced instruments and pull-out switches are typical of the German industry at the time.

A 1936 Frazer-Nash BMW with a British built pillarless saloon. This is the Type 315 known here as the Type 40.

A 1937 Whittingham and Mitchell open sports on the Type 55 (319) Frazer-Nash BMW seen here in a Coventry Cup Trial.

The two-door type (320 and 321)
saloon. This had the 1971 cc
45 bhp six-cylinder engine and was
in production from 1936 to 1940 —
not in itself one of the more beautiful
models.
The near-side view of the
straightforward 2 litre engine
— note the ignition control (no
Bowden cables here) that went to
a push-pull lever on the dash.
The off-side of the same engine;
but in the car, showing the
distinctive manifolding and the sump
breather running to the valve cover.

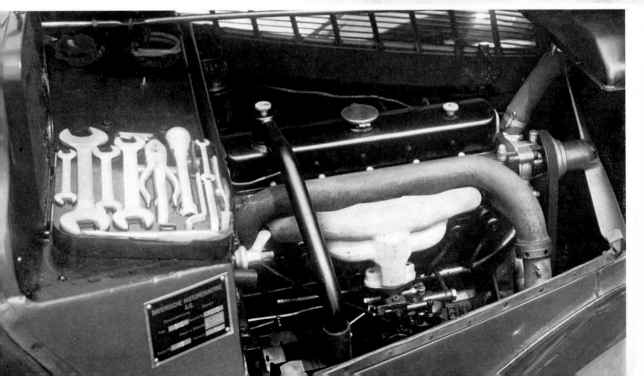

Practical rather than handsome —
the handbrake is interesting and
better than the post war umbrella —
the finish and layout are very typical
of German cars of the period.

Its very good publicity; but the boot
wasn't as big as all that and the
business of loading it from inside the
car made the job far from easy.

The pale grey striped cloth was very
smooth to the touch and universal,
regardless of the outside colour.

As soon as you get four-doors the appearance is much improved. Above is an early 326 with unusual solid disc wheels, while below is the more usual car with perforated wheels. With this car BMW went into direct competition with the small 'Merc'.

The line of the two-door cabriolet on the 326. Although not really very different from the 320 saloon with which, of course, it shared most of its pressings; it is a great deal better looking. The well padded hoods of German Cabriolets are fine until you try to open them up, when sheet bulk spoils the whole effect (the lower car is not the same model being a late version of the $1\frac{1}{2}$ litre).

The Front Suspension of the 326. It was this design as much as anything that brought the BMW to public acclaim, giving it a smooth ride and good road manners, which had up to that time often been very desperate things.

The dash-board of the 320 cabriolet on the opposite page — evident signs of smartening up.

The interior of the 320 Cabriolet showing the construction of the seats and the rear-opening door. This does not betoken a sudden awareness of safety factors, for later cars went back to front-opening doors as a convenience factor!

To prove the point here is the 321 Cabriolet with the door reversed — in all other respects it is almost identical to the other car.

Two views of a streamline saloon on what is thought to be a 326 chassis. It was exhibited at the Berlin Show in February 1938, the coachbuilder being Autenreith.

CHAPTER FIVE

The immortals

It is not given to many motor manufacturers, great or small, to make and market a really immortal motor car. Bugatti yes; and a select band of lunatics and perfectionists together with a mere handful of manufacturers. Even then some of the final count will be in dispute; but no-one is likely to gainsay the inclusion of the 328 BMW.

Its undoubted excellence as a motor car is, surprisingly, a little beside the point; for its real impact was the fact that it changed the face of the sports car in just the same way as Mercedes and Auto-Union changed the Grand Prix vehicle — and on nothing like the same resources. Up to the time the BMW swept the field the sports car had had a quite definite image — harsh and uncompromising. Cart springs, vestigal mudguards, noise, vibration and above all fun, coupled with road behaviour far in advance of the family saloon (which was not in those days so difficult to achieve). Sportsmen held that any diminution of the hard (literally) facts of sporting motor cars, would produce nothing less loathsome than Bunny Tubbs *bete noir* the Morris Ten-Six Cunard Tourer!

Suddenly all this thinking went by the board, for here was something that was unquestionably a sports car — after but a single season the records showed it — that was quiet and comfortable, softly sprung (well anyway by comparison) and generally much nearer a "roadster" than anyone at the time would care to admit. The shape too had changed — true it owed something to the previous $1\frac{1}{2}$ litre sports car and a little more to German design thinking in general; but anything further from a current Aston-Martin or a Frazer-Nash it would be hard to imagine.

Its two-litre engine broke new ground with an unusual, but not unique, system of valve operation; and the general advances in metalurgy as Europe worked its way towards its next war was put to good purpose to provide high output — BMW, of course, being in the aeroplane business.

It would be tidy, from an historical point of view, if the car had been an absolute loner; but since in a way it grew out of the 327 it was natural that the longer chassis should be offered with the advanced 328 engine. Here was a completely touring car of particularly attractive appearance powered by the competition engine — a car which later gave birth to the Bristol. In fact, the things that the 328 BMW started were to give rise to so many post-war delights in one way and another, that it can be said with absolute truth that very few cars indeed have had such an impact on the motoring scene as did this one.

It would be ungracious to suggest that the present day BMW success is derived solely from this one model — for the present cars stand in their own right; but what a start they had — if being born with a silver spoon in your mouth is an expression that still has any meaning, then in the Automobile world it must apply to today's BMWs.

There now needs to be a curious little postscript to this chapter; for, just as the war was about to engulf Western Civilisation, BMW produced a new touring car in the shape of the 3.5 litre Type 335. This was a straight throw at the Mercedes scene and is said, in some quarters, to have been aimed mostly at the British Market. However, by the time it got into production there was no British Market, and precious little market of any kind. The company only made 410 of them, so like the biggest fish in the fishermans story, as far as most of us are concerned, it was one that got away.

Perhaps this is the moment to add a word about the now almost mythical Frazer-Nash BMWs. In the first place, of course, they were plain BMWs for all the little "hints" in the very willing motoring press of the day to the effect that they were going to be built in Great Britain. True, since cars in those days had chassis, and small coachbuilders abounded, there were some British bodies; but by far the greater number of cars were just right-hand drive BMWs with altered badges.

There was some difference in nomenclature, the rather complex three figure model types of the manufacturers were replaced by Frazer-Nash with numbers relating to horsepower, i.e. Type 40 for the 315. They gave this up when it came to the 328, as its fame reached these shores before the cars.

It was a good ploy. Frazer-Nash was a good name and the BMW was a good car — unhappily Great Britains' relations with their country of origin were not, at that time, in very good fettle. Anything, therefore, which would soften the blow and help a man to feel the German car he was buying was in fact an *Anglo-German* car was, at least from a sales point of view, good sense.

Perhaps the most elegant of the bunch and the inspiration for the much less good-looking Bristol of post war years. This starts life as the 327 coupé with the "ordinary" 2 litre push-rod engine. Later it becomes available with the 328 engine from the sports car and gets called the 327/28. There is no apparent difference and even this photograph is captioned both ways by the BMW archive. There is an interesting door problem here too, for the drop head model has its doors opening the other way as can be seen overleaf.

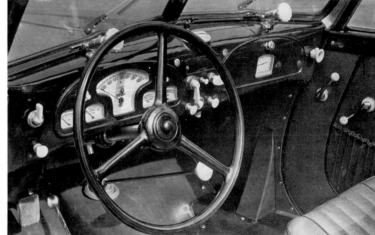

IIA-56871
D

And this is the drop head. The dark car above is claimed to be a 327 and the two-tone one like the coupé on the previous page could be either. Those with Sherlock Holmes instincts will take a close look at fuel filler caps; but as the bodies were built-out in small numbers that might not be so significant. At all events it was a very lovely car and is fast becoming (along with its immediate relations) a collectors piece.

A post war restoration. The wings have been more than a little changed the bumpers are "wrong". Traffic indicators have been fitted front and rear — the latter being from the first of the post war cars. The original head-lamp outlines have been altered and now house some more legally acceptable illumination.

A special 328 on the same chassis as the sports car, with what must have been one of the first "hard-tops" to be seen — the modifications are by Wendler.

On the previous page are three
views of the magic 328 engine
with its complicated cross-over
push rods giving a hemispherical
head with tiny 10 mm plugs buried
in the middle. A special spanner,
burnt hands and bad language were
the order of the day if they had to
come out in a hurry.

Shots of the immortal 328 showing
its admirable lines and its common-
sense design features. Certainly not
all the cars had the special driver's
seat and many people removed the
rear "spats" before they got
damaged. The folding V screen
went down (as of necessity) in two
parts; but the car could be used
with one down and a tonneau in place.

A special lightweight version about to leave Isleworth for a stint at Brooklands.

A car over which there has been much controversy. One of the 1940 Mille Miglia cars as it arrived in Great Britain after the war with a benevolent Gregor Grant presiding, hand in pocket, behind the windscreen. On the opposite page the car as now restored by Michael Bowler seen at the Nurburg Ring in August 1974 with a clutch of beauties behind him.

Again the real Mille Miglia car seen above at Silverstone in 1974 and below a sister car in the actual event. It is quite clear that these cars are different from the car shown by BMW immediately after the war as a "Mille Miglia" car.

The two closed Mille Miglia cars
— which as the photographs show
were somewhat different. The car
at the top which won the race also
ran at Le Mans with an additional
headlamp fixed in front of the
radiator. It may seem to be labouring
a point; but the company was still
unable to decide which way to hang
a door!

The "false" Mille Miglia car. Not as false as all that because it was made in Turin during the war and was to be the BMW entry in the first post war Mille Miglia had the other side won. However, as in motor racing, there is an unpredictable element in war and things did not turn out entirely as planned. But the car went on show as a Mille Miglia car which in a way it was.

This elegant (but very BMW) four-door cabriolet is on the almost mythical 3 litre type 335. Apart from size it is very difficult to distinguish from the 2 litre models; but it is evidently bigger and the bonnet louvres are distinctive (see over leaf).

Two views of the standard 335 saloon — said to be aimed at the British Market but more likely to have been aimed at Stuttgart-unter-Turkheim. Again the distinctive louvres and wings more heavily swaged. The neat luggage carrier in the lower photograph is more typical of Germany in general than of BMW in particular.

CHAPTER SIX

The first fruits of success

It seems very unlikely that the kudos from the early Eisenach essays, or the modest successes of the Wartburgs and Dixis, rubbed off on to the newly successful BMW company; but with the background and the ambitions of the company's directors particularly Popp (whose daughter Erica had married Richard Seaman only just before his tragic crash at Spa) was ernest enough of the firms intent.

The introduction of the $1\frac{1}{2}$ litre sports car was a clear beginning, although in fact the company had already with the 13/15PS (their own first development of the Dixi) gained a class victory with their team in the 1929 Austrian Alpine Trial. The 315/1 with its three carburettors won the team prize in the 1934 Alpine Trial which among other things led to the co-operation with the Frazer Nash company in the marketing of BMWs in the United Kingdom. A similar car was later offered as the 319/1 and also had its share of success.

The real triumph arrived with the 328 which had been heralded by Ernest Henne (the BMW world-record motor-cyclist) winning the 1936 Eifelrennen in a sports version of the 326 which was introduced at the Berlin Show that year. When it did arrive the 328 had, as a production model, an 80 bhp engine and a top speed of 100 mph, and in the official works versions these figures were much improved. A considerable stir was caused at Brooklands by Sammy Davis who set out in one of the newly imported cars to do a hundred miles in the hour, and succeeded easily — for a two litre sports car in those days it was a quite remarkable feat.

For the three years or so before the outbreak of the war BMW had things all their own way in the two-litre class with successes at Le Mans, the 24-hour race at Spa, the Tourist Trophy, the Mille Miglia not to mention events nearer home such as the Avus and the German Grand Prix. They won an event at Bucharest called a Grand Prix and the Grand Prix des Frontieres as well as Benito Mussolini's oddball political event the Tobruk-Benghazi-Tripoli.

They then won outright the 1940 Mille Miglia (which was an "abreviated" event which did not use the proper course) with Hushke von Hanstein and Baumer at the wheel at an average speed of 103.5 mph. The aftermath of this success has been with us for a long time, as just after the war BMW paraded a "Mille Miglia" car which was *not* the car which won the Mille Miglia! The BMW museum car is a mid-war effort at what would have been in other circumstances the post-war car. The real Mille Miglia cars are well documented in photographs here, so that there can be no doubt; and Michael Bowler in his own magazine has given all the chapters and all the verses for those who feel they need more than the captions on the following pages reveal — which is thought to be almost everything!

It was the little 1½ litre which started things off — and here is one of the first in the 1937 Torquay Rally.
With the arrival of the 328 things began to hum. The car was rather surprisingly just as much at home in the British reliability trial. Here is H. C. Hunter on Darracott Hill in the 1939 Lands End.

But obviously the cars were at their best on the track. This is the Crystal Palace — where the advantages of a two litre on handicap are all too obvious.

The Frazer Nash BMW team for the 1939 R.A.C. Rally lined up by the Aquarium at Brighton. Left to Right. Fane, Johnson and Abecassis.

Good looks rewarded early. The Eastbourne Concours d'Elegance where Mrs. Fane (with husband on passengers side) won the £501-£1000 class for open sports cars.

The 1937 TT, run at Donington Park. Bira was third overall and won the two-litre class.

S. C. H. 'Sammy' Davis, then sports editor of the Autocar, at the wheel of the special lightweight 328 in which he covered 102.227 miles in the hour at Brooklands.

The start of the 1938 German Grand Prix for Sports Cars. The 2 litre class was a BMW benefit. Not since the early days of Bugatti, had a starting-grid been so dominated by one make.

By 1939 the Le Mans circuit was already beginning to look as it does to-day with the two storey pits and the revetted banks. Below right, the BMW is followed by a 12-cylinder Lagonda designed by W. O. Bentley, and behind that the winning Bugatti driven by J. P. Wimille.

BMW made a big effort at the 1939 Le Mans race. Their entries consisted of an Italian bodied streamlined coupé, which was later to win the 1940 Mille Miglia, and two ordinary 328s. Prince Schaumburg-Lippe and Wenscher drove the coupé, Roese and Heinemann, and Brien and Scholz the two open 328s. The cars finished 5th, 7th and 9th.

In the upper picture the Briem/Richter open car leads the Brudes/Roese example round the Cremona hairpin in the 1940 Mille Miglia, while below, Hushke Von Hanstein takes the chequered flag in the slimmer of the two closed cars.

CHAPTER SEVEN

The sincerest form of flattery

At the end of Europe's second war, we know the BMW company was in a bad state — just how bad is hard to guess. If the allies had decided, there and then, to do as much for Germany as they later did, they would perhaps have been busy getting the Bavarian Motor Works rebuilt instead of having it hacked to pieces. Had they done so, the course of history would have been a good deal different and it seems unlikely that the Bristol Aeroplane company would have been able to embark on making what was in effect the pre-war 328, modified, so that however much better it was in certain details, it was a lot worse in looks.

To begin with, the factory at Eisenach where our story started, was in the Russian Zone and there was little that could be done about that. Predictably the Russian Authorities decided, without more than a few months hesitation, that anything Bristol could do they could do better—and that they had both the men and the machines for doing it.

The first EMW (Eisenach Motor Works) appeared as soon as 1945 — the BMW company, as far as the Russians were concerned, having been "nationalised". The management was in the hands of something called Awtovelo and was export orientated. The first cars were plain BMWs and even the old radiator badge was used, but by 1952 the EMWs were appearing based on the pre-war 2 litres, the 321 being exactly the same, and the 327 as near as makes no odds. Later came the 340/2 based on the 326 but with a different front (the old pressing had been messed about) and then there were some Formula 2 racing cars; but by 1955 the works was renamed Automobilewerk Eisenach and the BMW copies ceased along with our interest.

Much more fun were the Veritas cars, mostly because they were primarily sports and competition models. The company was formed in 1948 by the ex-BMW employees under the direction of Ernst Loof. The old 328 BMW engine was used in a tubular frame which could carry either two seater or "monoposto" bodies, providing sports or Formula 2 possibilities. There were also some road cars and a $1\frac{1}{2}$ litre version, using the 328 engine with the stroke reduced, which was said to develop 100 bhp.

Later, the company progressed to a point where it had its own engines made by Heinkel and our interest in them therefore ceases. That original 328 engine was so good, and so successful in Bristol and other cars, that one wonders just how splendid a vehicle might have come out of the factory after the war if only the Control Commission had been a little more far-sighted. Imagination boggles and one can only fly to Robert Sothey's frightful poem "After Blenheim" for explanation:

> And many a childing mother then
> And new born baby died:
> But things like that, you know, must be
> At every famous victory.

A post war special built by Polensky (who subsequently became known for his Monopole cars). It is basically a 328 but with a number of Citroen parts in the suspension. Said to have been faster than the Veritas.

One of the so called fake Mille Miglia cars. Some sources say more than a dozen of these were built; but they can have fooled no-one; and incidentally where are they now?

The Veritas engine — a photograph which leaves little doubt about its origins.

A 2 litre Veritas — one of the sports, as opposed to "Grand Prix" models.

The Formula 2 Veritas (sometimes called Veritas-Meteor) This is Karl Kling in the 1950 German G.P. (Formula 2).

More Veritas examples. Above, an early open two-seater looking very Spitfire-like and below, one of the standard saloons which become a successful small run production.

Two Veritas drop-heads with the characteristic, but not very lovely front. The lower car is the long wheelbase version, for once not looking better in light paint.

The Veritas Scorpion in its 1950 guise with an engine developed and made by Heinkel — only its ancestry fits it for these pages.

The Elva BMW G.T. 160 which made its debut at Earls Court in 1964. It was not a one-off but very few were made.

CHAPTER EIGHT

As a Phoenix from the flames

If too young for memory to serve, one still does not need very much imagination to see that the end of the war was the end of BMW — or at least a fair imitation of it. The plant was dismantled by the military authorities — the Eisenach works (where all the cars had been built) was in the Russian Zone. The Bristol Aeroplane Company were making their idea of what the 327/8 should have been, and there wasn't any money anyway.

1949 saw 9450 examples of the 250 cc motor bike very readily sold, the big bikes followed and in 1951 the first car. Not, as one might have supposed, the austerity model in the manner of the Volkswagen but a luxury car with a two litre engine based on the pre-war designs. The outside was an up-to-date reworking of the pre-war BMW line; and the car was well made, luxuriously finished and full of hope — it was also full of room for development, for the company saw themselves even in those dark hours, as people who were going to make good, high-class cars.

It followed naturally therefore that they should in the fullness of time replace the two-litre with the first V8 to come out of post-war Germany. They were properly proud of this effort and the two particularly splendid sports cars that came out of it and form the basis of a later chapter; but they were really in advance of both their time and their circumstances. The day of the "middle luxury" car had not yet come, so the demand was small. In consqeuence production was small —too small to make sense—and the price, in consequence, too much for too many and probably not enough for a few. The red light had stopped blinking on the boardroom wall and had gone on for keeps.

However, enthusiastic as they may have been, the board were not blind to the position and plans were afoot for a small (but very interesting) car to fit the needs of the day. No one on the present staff knows very much about it; and it remains one of those mysteries rather like the small Rover that it so closely resembles. Owing much to the pre-war Fiat "Topolino" it had the external markings of the BMW marque and would have been a pretty little thing if it had ever seen the light of the showroom. As to its mechanicals there is one picture in the archives which "may have been" its engine — clearly derived from the motor-cycle unit, it was a fairly obvious beginning; but there are those who believe there were plans for a four cylinder unit.

It is a matter of some wonder to some of us at least, that where a firm possess their own museum, things do not find their way into it; but if they did there would, perhaps, be no scope for books such as this.

The first post-war BMW did not appear until the Frankfurt Show in 1951 which gave the designers a little time for thought. When it did appear the 501 was of advanced design and although fitted with what was in effect the pre-war 2 litre engine, the chassis had obviously been designed for better things. The suspension was sophisticated and the massive tubular chassis light. Concession to current fashion was the steering column gear change; but apart from that it was clearly a new conception.

The styling department did a good job of preserving the old BMW image while at the same time going along with current thought. It was to be a big comfortable car, and it looked it.

In due course improvements were made — particularly added power from the engine — up from 65 bhp to 72 bhp — and minor improvements to the coachwork. Here is the 501 A. The absence of chromium moulding on the waistline distinguishes them from the later V 8s.

The *interior shows how strong the American influence was at that time — even down to the steering column gear change.*

The *round and not very big looking BMW boot would hold more than you might have imagined. All the same the circular hat box is just not going to go in.*

The four-seater cabriolet was soon added to the range, and a very handsome car it turned out to be. If nothing else this model points up the fact that if BMW was to survive, the luxury car market would need to grow.

Two special bodies. Top a four-door "state" car employing panels from both the four-door saloon and the standard convertible. Below one of the very rare special bodies on a post war BMW. This saloon by Farina very much on the lines of the then current Alfa Romeo and Lancia models. It never became a production car.

The projected post war "baby". Very clearly BMW in shape but owing a lot to the pre-war Fiat "Topolino", this little car never went into production and little is now known about it. Even when it comes to the engine, on the left, all that can be said is that it is "probably" the engine. It is thought there were others. Whether it was front or rear wheel drive seems open to question; but shape would suggest a conventional layout.

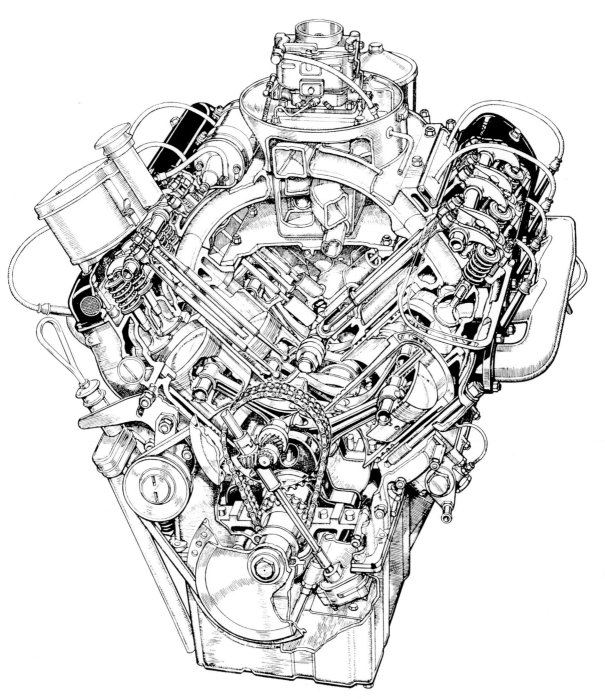

Cut away drawing of the first V 8 to come out of Germany after the war. The 2½ litre introduced in 1955. It was later expanded to 3½ litres for the sports cars.

The chassis of the 502 showing how readily the V8 fitted in; but otherwise it was the same as the previous car — the whole being a clearly intended development. The same goes for the car itself seen ghosted below.

The *502 V8* looking to all intents and purposes the same as the previous car with small differences of trim. As a shape it tended to look better in light colour or when elongated as below in a model made specially for Chancellor Adenauer and termed *505*.

The interior of the V8 — an interesting comparison with the six-cylinder on page 103.
The rear of the V8 with appropriate insignia (an American habit no-one apparently has the courage to lose). The picture also shows how the waist moulding was dealt with on a design that did not originally have one.

The front end – road lamps which replace the winkers are the only give-away – it was time enough after he had passed you, for you to know it was a V8.

One of the later dashboards with the two spoked wheel borrowed from the sports cars – but still the loathsome column change.

Two special designs with no credit for the coachbuilders; but memory of the Sunbeam Venezia (which was never marketed in Great Britain) would suggest Vignale for the upper car and possibly Graber for the lower.

CHAPTER NINE

Hard times

Faced with the problems of a failing market in large cars, with the evident costs of tooling up to make a small one, and what might be called a collapse in motor cycles, the BMW directorate took a surprising but not unthinking course, and one which their predecessors had taken twice before.

In Italy the Iso company had produced a "bubble car" which made a certain amount of sense. With three wheels, a door which opened in the front and a fairly beastly 200 cc two stroke engine, it clearly filled a need. With motor-cycle experience behind them, and no great development costs to face, BMW took a licence to make the cars in Germany and to fit their own more powerful four stroke engine. It turned the tide a little and things must have looked better still when an English company (Isetta of Great Britain) took a licence to build them here. The run in Germany which amount to some 150,00 or more of the machines lasted from 1954 until 1963, and even then they were not finished with it for a four wheel version of the same idea went on to the market as the BMW 600. This proved to be less attractive and in the end the exercise cannot be called a commercial success.

The cars were notable, at least on this side of the Channel, for their publicity impact more than anything else; and all the famous and some of the infamous were photographed with them to a point where one might have supposed that the kind of popular success enjoyed by the Mini was not far away, at all events it was too far away to be grasped, and the company faced considerable financial difficulties.

Something needed to be done and done fast. Plans were put in hand to produce a much more conventional small car using their own quite excellent motor-cycle engine; and indeed, when it came this car transformed their market situation — at least temporarily. However before that comes into the story we need to take a last look at the luxury cars — the swan song of the ideas that grew out of the 328 and some of the most lovely cars marketed in their period.

The BMW Isetta. This was, of course, a design bought from the Italian Iso company who had been making it with a two-stroke unit. BMW wisely decided to fit a four-stroke of their own and offered the car with a choice of either 250 or 300 cc. It was made under licence (from BMW) in Great Britain — in the old railway sheds at Brighton Station. It was imported into America by the Fadex Commercial Corporation, who are responsible for the Cary Grant publicity shot. While not concerned with the Great Days of Hollywood this does show very well how the car worked. (There are three pedals by the way — two on the left of the steering column as you look at it). The engine was mounted on the (British) off-side and the ventilating louvres can be seen.

The British M...

As if obliged to compete with Mr. Grant the British Company secured the services of a pretty but unnamed lady and of Mr. Stirling Moss to lend her support.

Not only a star's car; but a star in its own right, as the official transport for Peter Ustinov (the head of a mythical Republic) who had just made a stirring speech to the United Nations. The film, Romanoff & Juliette was made in 1961, so things have not changed all that much.

The small size of the Isetta limited its appeal — and numbers were what the company desperately needed — so the 600 was produced with no "Isetta" reference at all. Indeed it was a BMW conception. With four seats and three doors (the front end was straight Isetta) it was a fascinating little car; but it failed to fascinate enough people to keep the accountants happy.

CHAPTER TEN

Swan song of delight

It might have seemed more logical to include the last of the V8 BMWs in an earlier chapter, along with the saloon versions of the same cars. They seem so special, however, that little excuse is needed to separate them from the herd and to treat them as the special things they were intended to be.

One does not easily see them in perspective to-day, for they represent the kind of car that has now almost gone; and lingers on only less gloriously in the Triumph Stag. — They were what can only be called "roadsters" — and that in a European rather than in an American context — and certainly nothing to do with Indianapolis where that same word had yet another meaning.

To most minds the roadster comes out of America in general, and Hollywood in particular; with a broad front seat a dickey, with a square hole twixt one and t'other where golf clubs could be stowed. In the more expensive versions, painted white, it was a Hollywood car.

In Europe we had not much regard for such things; for, fast and powerful as they were, they offered zero roadholding and lacked much of the charm of the well made car. Mercedes were perhaps pre-eminent in changing all that though a good many other people from Hispano-Suiza to Horch had a hand in it. Late in the thirties elegant couples were pictured in advertisements, complete with aircraft in the background and linen flying helmets on their heads, flashing round what looked like a cross between Ascot and Templehoff — and after the war the image stuck.

Of all the German roadsters the BMW was the most handsome — and to keep it up to the minute there was a hard-top. It had real performance and yet we all knew in fact it was not a sports car. Its earlier brother also sported some special coachwork, although the marque as a whole never became a favourite with outside body-builders — perhaps overall production numbers were. so small that the factory discouraged them.

In the end, however you look at it, the 507 held in the mid-fifties a place very near to that of the 328 in its day, and played a very great part in creating the image to which the company was able to return when times were less hard and some more capital had been found. It is one of the astonishing things in the BMW story that the company, despite its changes in finance and management, despite a world war and its aftermath, has always had an image of the kind of car it wanted to make. It has returned to that image no matter how often external forces have driven it off course. Perhaps therein lies the secret of its appeal.

The *503 coupé was a handsome car by any standards, in retrospect very reminiscent of the Lagonda. Made between 1955 and 1960 it had a V8 engine giving 140 hp and, it was claimed, did 190 kph.*

The drop-head, particularly with the head down, was even better looking, though below the waist it was identical. A single colour certainly helped. It was the beginning of the return to luxury for many people whose immediate past had been devastated by war — as such it made an impression probably out of proportion to its merit.

The 502 prototype — a one off 1954/55 design-exercise looking very like the earliest Veritas; but clearly leading to other things.

And here are the other things—"straight off the drawing board" as you might say. The first of the 507's and as much a classic as the 327/8. It is one of the few cases where the hard top really works, in that the car seems as complete with it as without it.

Two more shots of what is truly one of the world's most beautiful cars — better in one colour (above) than in the more usual White and Black (with red upholstery) seen below. Not really a sports car of the old school, it nevertheless had standards of roadholding and performance which in its time made it as fast and pleasurable as most.

Cause and effect. Above, an early drawing from the Bertone Studio of the projected 3200 CS coupé and below the car as it appeared at the Frankfurt Show. The V8 engine now produced 160 hp and the claimed maximum was 200 kph. Not really a replacement for the 507 it showed the way the sales were going; the kind of car people were looking for. It was introduced in 1963 roughly two years after the 507 had been withdrawn.

Two more views of the 3200 CS coupé — though in the top shot it may suffer some competition. The neat detail work shows well in the lower photograph; but the car looks what it is — an Italian design of the period.

This two seater appeared at the 1959 Turin Show at a time when Vignale had the TR3-Italia in production. It is so nearly the same car that one wonders what they were at; but it must have been very nice even though it never became a serious competitor to the Triumph.

CHAPTER ELEVEN

Looking for salvation

Things continued to go down hill for the company — the big cars, if they sold at all, sold in too few numbers to make any kind of sense however much the horns of overheads were drawn in. The Isetta was all right as far as it went; but it never got more than half-way to the bank. Motor-cycles were at their lowest ebb ever — so, little man, what now?

Having a very decent horizontally opposed twin which could easily go into a car was, at least, a point of departure. To make a car that had a certain BMW charm (which to be honest the Isetta did not) would be another step. Europe at the time was bursting its sides with economy models, few of which had any real appeal so here was a chance. Out of that chance the 700 was born.

To all outward appearances a Triumph Herald — but lets just say great minds think alike — the little bike engine fitted neatly into the back and as rear engine, rear wheel drive was then almost an accepted norm for small cars no eyebrows need be raised about that. Planned as a very ordinary day-to-day transport sort of car, it soon emerged as having very considerable sporting possibilities — greatly to the pleasure of its manufacturers.

The 697 cc twin developed 40 bhp in the so called sports version; and it did quite well in the touring classes of international rallies and to some extent on the circuits. Enough at all events for the company to embark on the production of the 700 RS which had a tubular space-frame and a shortened wheelbase. In this the engine was placed in front of the rear axle (instead of behind it as in the other models) and was persuaded to develop 70 bhp at 8,000 rpm. It was, in its way, quite a formidable competition car.

For the rest the little closed coupé and its drop-head equivalent, looking if anything even more Herald like, continued to sell well. In an effort to gild the lily some rather bizarre patches of colour were added to the sides, rather in the same way as efforts had been made to jazz-up the fading Austin and Morris ranges some years before.

From the companies' point of view it turned the tide to some extent, adding nearly five million marks to the turnover in 1960; but it was not enough. All the same it bridged the gap until the new four-cylinder car could be got ready for the market, and the latest and most successful period of BMW history could begin.

Within a very short time of introduction the 700 had begun to make its appearance in competition. It was before International Rallies became quite so desperately professional; and there was a good place for small sporting saloons despite a certain tendency for the tail to wag the dog on icy roads! On the other hand in the Acropolis there were at least no boiling troubles, and in any event the cars were quick to service and very robust.

Delighted by more mundane successes the factory decided to build a mid-engined model using a good many 700 parts (enough for Advertisement) and a good many quite special parts (enough for Victory). It never became a world beater but it had a presentable record.

And along with the Minis (and almost everyone else) the little 700 was soon seen on the circuits as well.

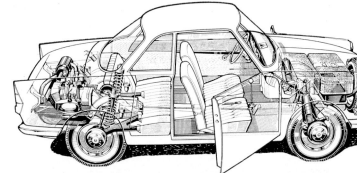

*If the 600 was not the looked for
success it might have been at least
it provided thinking for a neat
small car using the motor cycle
engine and the 700 was the result.*

Good looking and practical —
though less pleasant when jazzed-up
— it was just the sort of car for its
time. A far cry from some of the
splendours near the managements
heart; but it changed the companies'
finances and made way for the better
things to come.

Being Bavarian the beloved cabriolet
was never far away — and it looked
very well. The rear seats in either
model were really only for children as
the hood made some inroads.
Fighting for their lives at the time,
the press department waxed very
eloquent "The new elegant BMW 700
cabrio meets the dream of many
automobile enthusiasts. Performance
40 hp top speed 135 kph. With few
manipulations the Cabrio is
transformed into a well heated and
well closed automobile free of draft."

And in the same vein. "Driving in the open air with this lovely and sporty BMW 700 Cabrio makes much pleasure. It is a richly equipped car of first class with extraordinary driving qualities which captivates also the lady on the steering wheel" . . . like they said.

This is the saloon which had a slightly higher roof and a less pronounced slope to the rear window giving, of course, more space inside. The engine and its accessories were neatly done and as can be seen from the bottom picture it was very habitable inside even if not lush.

CHAPTER TWELVE

The turn of the tide

It was at the 1961 Frankfurt Show that the new 1500 cc BMW made its debut, and with it came the beginnings of the new era in the company's affairs. It was a going-back in many ways, back to the little boxy saloon of the mid-thirties, which had done so much to bring the firm to pre-eminence before the war. On the surface just another small saloon — uglier than a good many, simpler than some; but almost unique in its motoring appeal. It is a kind of charm almost impossible to assess; but looking back there is little doubt that when a rather ordinary duckling turns out to be a swan beneath the skin, the public reaction always seems very marked.

Like little Topsy, of course, it just 'growed'—and by 1966 there was a two-litre version that went like the wind, with enough extra equipment available on some models for all and sundry to know that the wind was blowing through Christmas Trees. Four-doors came as a matter of course; and, as if to put the seal of success on everything they touched, the company was able to announce in 1966 that they had made a quarter of a million motor bikes since the end of the war. It was also, anyway by one system of reckoning, the company's 50th anniversary; and just to show that time had not blunted their imagination they went and bought the Glas motor works and made, for a short while, some interesting V8 cars.

Then followed the first of the post-war six, a 2½ litre car with a handsome four-door saloon. This engine was later expanded to three litres where it, of course, gained power but lost a little charm. To follow the Saloon came a marvellous Coupé, to put the company back where they had let go of the "luxuswagen" scene with the demise of the 3200Cs V8 about the time of the little 700.

Then came a new saloon body shell in what is now known as the "5" series — owing something to Alfetta, not to mention Morris Marina, thinking. This is not to criticise but just to point the fashion; for the new Ford Escort has gone the same way, so that individuality is hard to come by these days even in the august fields now inhabited by BMW — *Sic transit*.

But amid all the "executive models, and all the marketing of the upper-middle-class image, the sporting interest prevailed; and as we shall see in a later chapter not without considerable success. One offshoot of it was a number of slightly curious road cars, bedecked with spoilers back and front, striped like Joseph's technicolor coat, and in at least one instance with words painted across the front in reverse, so that unsuspecting persons glancing in their mirrors might be told, in thinly disguised terms "get out of the bloody way". This proved unpopular with all but the owners (who were probably unpopular anyway) and it was dropped.

After a long and in some ways troubled history, with a background of at least two really outstanding cars on either side of the war behind them, the firm seemed at last set on its course as one of the most distinguished manufacturers.

By the 1st January 1967 BMW had control of Glas — more to get to production space than anything else; but for a bit they went on selling and making Glas cars. Here is a product of the immediate take-over period with either a 1000 or 1300 engine. Nice but not BMW. Part of the reason for needing more space was the success of the 1500 cc cars (and its derivitives) which first appeared in 1962. This is the original 1500 cc four-door saloon.

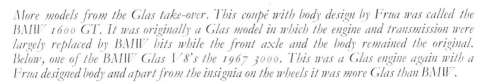

More models from the Glas take-over. This coupé with body design by Frua was called the BMW 1600 GT. It was originally a Glas model in which the engine and transmission were largely replaced by BMW bits while the front axle and the body remained the original. Below, one of the BMW Glas V8's the 1967 3000. This was a Glas engine again with a Frua designed body and apart from the insignia on the wheels it was more Glas than BMW.

The *1966 1600*, a straight development of the previous *1500*, and the beginning of a very long run indeed.

The *1600* drop-head (*1967*). All the usual BMW thinking going back to well before the war. Every two-door saloon has its drop-head half-brother.

The *1600* saloon in its "ti" version (*105* hp) showing some difference in the front grill.

The later type of standard 1800 Saloon — from 1968 onwards to 1970.

The earlier 1800 saloon in production from 1963 until the introduction of the model above in 1968.

The 1971 version of the same car — the most obvious change being in the wheels. The engine remained virtually unaltered through all this time giving 90 bhp.

The 2000 CA/CS coupé. In fact the big coupé with the 2000 cc four-cylinder engine. From this time, 1965, onwards BMW were given to swapping around all the available bits to make a great variety of models.

And, of course, adding goodies to produce models such as this 2000 cc "Tilux" saloon of 1966/68.

This is the ordinary 2000 cc four-cylinder four-door of 1966 — available from 1971 onwards with a 1.8 litre engine as the BMW 1800.

Also from the 1971 period this two-door version which eventually becamed dubbed the "two series" here in its 1802 form.

Then came the "hatchback" craze; and the Reliant followed by Volvo with split folding rear seats. This is the BMW answer in its later 1973 guise.

And in its earlier 1600 or 2000 cc 1971 form. Apart from the wheel centres there is almost no discernable difference.

Still held by many to be the nicest post-war BMW of them all. The 1968 2500 — the first of the six-cylinder range.

And in its 2.8 litre form the engine just not quite as silky, though obviously more powerful.

With shades of Bertone from the past, the 2800CS of 1968. Also as a 3 litre from 1971.

Another view of the coupé showing its very handsome lines. This is actually the 1971 3 litre.

And this the 1971 3 litre saloon.

The 3.0 CSL of 1973 in all its war paint. This boy-racer approach did BMW little credit, and was soon dropped — whatever merits it had on the track, or in the Kings Road, it had little to commend it in the magistrates court.

Three more shots of the two-door saloon in its final guise as part of the "02 Series". Available in 1602, 1802, and 2002 versions from 85 to 130 bhp. It goes directly back to the first of the four-cylinder 1500 cc cars and was for many years the mainstay of production. It is now replaced by the first of the Three series.

The 1971 2002 "til" — a combination of high performance and luxury in an effort to widen the choice in what was after all a fairly small range.

The 2002 Cabriolet. A rather complicated (and very expensive) essay in the drop-head idiom designed to give the currently acceptable, but usually hideous, fixed "roll bar" even when the car is open. Makes one sigh for some of the early drop-heads.

The 2002 Turbo. Less obviously boy-racer but very, very, quick. 170 bhp with turbo-charging. But all the same, not a thing of beauty though, no doubt, to many happy owners a joy for (nearly) ever.

A design exercise rather in the manner of the American manufacturers' "dream cars" — and certainly not intended for general production — try opening the doors against a busy pavement.

All the same some of the ideas, notably the dashboard and the front end treatment, were to find their way into the new "Three series" cars. And is it not very handsome?

To widen the scope and give a slightly smaller and more modern car, the "Five series" with either the four or the six-cylinder engines. Less distinctive, they filled a need, and paved the way for a "luxus" long wheelbase version of the older saloon seen below.

CHAPTER THIRTEEN

New lamps for old

Nothings stands still, least of all in the business of making motor cars; and the fact had to be faced that the four cylinder models; direct decendents of the original 1½ litre which had turned the firm back on the road to recovery, were getting long in the tooth. You cannot keep a car in production indefinitely unless, like Citroen, you make something that is way out at the start. And for all its virtues the little BMW which made its debut at Frankfurt in 1961 was not way out; and so by the mid seventies it was no longer all that remarkable; and some features, such as the ventilation, were not up to anyones' scratch, least of all BMW's.

So, with a certain amount of muddle about release dates. the new generation of small BMWs crept into public view during the hot summer. Known as the 3-Series and at prices some four percent or so above the cars they replaced which had become known as the "02 range" (1502, 1602, 1802 and 2002) they were not very different in their mechanicals. To try and call the operation a "face-lift" would be to do it a great deal less than justice; but as is so often the case these days you either get the old works in a new body or new works in an old body — it seems almost as if the day of the new car has finally disappeared.

Even on the mechanical side the company could claim some feathers to put in its cap. With compression ratios down and power up, the cars used two star petrol and yet had reduced nitrous oxides in the exhaust. Bigger radiators, larger, and therefore we hope quieter, exhaust systems, efforts to reduce engine noise all add up to better and more civilised cars.

The bodies were quite new — owing a little in general shape to the 5-Series cars and a good deal to modern Turin ideas (though BMW give no credits in that direction) they are only some four inches longer than their predecessors. There is a heavy accent on safety, which we now have to accept as necessary to sales if not to salvation; but for all that there is the well known, and for many people well loved, BMW sense of light and air. There is a new and proper through-flow ventilation system and the new dashboard and the layout of the instruments are all that a motorist could desire, being full of function and free of fuss.

Alas we shall be unlikely to see custom bodies on these or any other BMWs in the years to come; but if standard cars for standard men are all we are to be allowed, we can perhaps be grateful for the standards of the Bavarian Motor Works who manage to make standardisation that much more acceptable.

The new "Three series". 316, 320 and 320i, these replace this year (1975) the war-horse two-door four-cylinder cars which have served so well. An up-market image is sought by good lines and good equipment (even a tool kit), and the overall outline fits in well with the "Five series", cars.

Front end treatment reminiscent of the Turbo shows itself here to good advantage. A lot less obvious is the possibility of running on two-star petrol, at least on some of the models.

An engine is an engine these days and overcrowding too often the order of the day; but the dashboard does clearly spring from the ideas expressed in the turbo — and good ideas at that.

The return to
thing it was a
they did their
Munich. Thei
introduction
try them in ra

The first re
507. Driven
and made the
them the 700
soon became
class of many
bits in it; but

In 1966 a
special head (
260 bhp and
following ye
reduced to 16
225 bhp whe
engine went
versions — a

Then the
dropped and
2. They drop
coque by the
and did fairly
and Quester
one Hockhei
call it a day.

In the field
the day ever
have been m
most is that
of their riva
more worth
models have
inclined.

Success in
sold BMWs
years of succ

The interior of the "Three series" is neat but not gaudy — indeed it makes in both colour and texture, an interesting comparison with the pre-war cars. Vision and safety have been well cared for.

The new
3·3 Li, is th
the better
and d

Centre a
or 63
March
which fu
appeal
keeping

Perhaps it was the pre-war record,
or perhaps the availability of any big
car, that put the early post-war
saloons into competition. They were
unlikely vehicles but acquitted
themselves well, if without much
glory. They are seen here above, in the
1954 Monte, centre, on the Sestriere
rally with the famous round hotel in
the background and below, in France
during the 1954 Tulip where the neat
parking (not to mention the whitewall
tyres) seem to satisfy the Gendamerie.

Heuberger won the over 2000 cc class for touring cars in the '57 Mille Miglia. Seen here on the starting ramp. And below, an appearance was also entered in the Acropolis.

The *507 was clearly a car with competition possibilities. Here they are exploited by Robert Jenny in the '58 Mille Miglia where he won his class (Gran Turismo Speciale over 2000 cc) and by an un-named enthusiast in the Wallburg hill-climb in the following year.*

The new four-cylinder cars introduced in 1962 went immediately into competition as a natural thing. Here in the 1964 Monte one of them scuttles over the difficult Turini, while below, in the 13th Tour de France (1964) the competitors Count Emsiedel and Prince Metternich look happy enough at the start.

One of the earliest racing cars was this Lola fitted with a two litre BMW engine (left) and raced by Equipe Elva London with the support of Esso and Trojan-Elva; but still a private team run by Ernie Unger. The driver was Tony Lanfranchi seen here at Goodwood where he achieved a lap record.

Whitman's BMW in for service during the 1965 Monte showing, if nothing else, that BMW were taking their Rally effort very seriously.

Snetterton the same year with Lang on the right of Hahne in the middle of the picture, Allmer leaning against the bonnet of no. 55 and Miersch on the extreme left.

Nurburg 1966 — the six hours race. Falkenhausen and Hahne discussing the chances.

Swedish entrants in the 1966 Tulip. The man with the dark glasses evidently finds time pressing, and the British at least may get some glee from the Team Bee Pee sticker.

A line-up in the sunshine, in competition with Alfa-Romeo and Ford in the saloon car class.

All in all, 1966 was a good year for BMW. Here in the Spa 24 hours is Hahne anxiously waiting to take over from Ickx, coming in with the 2000 Ti, in which they won the event.

From 1966 onwards the company interested itself in single-seaters. Firstly above, with the Apfelbeck modified engine and the Brabham ex-formula I chassis. Then with the engine reduced to 1600 cc for Formula II in the Lola T100 chassis, and lastly on the following page Quester who with a 2 litre engine competed in the European Mountain Championship.

*Thruxton, Easter Monday 1970 the BMW team in the paddock with a fine line-up of names
— Hahne in particular played a massive part in BMW's competition effort, driving everything
everywhere.*

Two shots of the 1968 "Monti Berg Spider" hill-climb car. Fitted with the Apfelbeck engine it used a Lola T120 chassis and was usually driven by Dieter Quester who also used it occasionally, as here, on the circuit.

The 1967 "Eifel" Formula II race at the Nurbergring with Surtees leading the pack in his Lola BMW followed by Jim Clark in a Cosworth powered Lotus.

Another picture of the hill climb car driven by Quester on the circuit. — this time at Vienna where he won.

No one ever doubted the handling qualities of the small BMW, but few people have put them to so severe a test as Dieter Basche, seen here at Snetterton.

One of the 1970 team cars which represented the final phase in BMW's Formula 2 effort.

This picture and the two on the following page show the boy-racers in action. With 3.5 litre engines giving 430 bhp they were formidable machines. The prominent "Bavarian Motor Works" on the windscreens was not put there for the benefit of this book, but for the benefit of the watching American public. The caption of the last photograph coyly says "Boxenstop-Sekunden entscheiden" which shows that once you get into the spirit of the Boys Own Paper there's no stopping.

CHAPTER FIFTEEN

Two's Company

There was no leaving the motor cycles out of this book, even though it has not been the policy in this series to include anything but the cars, whatever else any particular manufacturer may have made. With BMW it is different. To begin with the major side of the firm began its interest in road vehicles with motor cycles; and it was only after the success of these that they cast about and began to concern themselves with the possibilities of four wheel production.

The company began when Gustav Otto set up his aeroplane factory at Munich, and was first expanded when he joined forces with Rapp in 1913. It was after the first world war, when the company had built a big reputation in the aeronautical field, that they set about making a motor-bike. It was a good machine; and advanced for its time; but the real magic was yet to come. The BMW bikes of to-day are quite astonishingly similar to the original machines. That is not to say that development over the years has not been both expert and necessary; but all in all the ideas of the first BMW are the ideas of to-day. It still has shaft drive and a horizontally opposed twin engine set across the frame. Springing still pays a vital part; and consecutive pictures of the front forks over the years show how hard they have been at work to secure perfection.

On the sporting side their successes have been very considerable. As solo machines they have held many records — including the world's record itself — and no less than 205 others; and as the first foreigner on a foreign machine "Schorsch" Meier won the 1939 TT.

But it is not as solos that we really think of BMWs, for in the field of sidecar events — surely the most exciting of all motor sports — they have totally dominated the scene for many years, clocking up no less than 14 wins in the TT since 1954 and in '73 they were declared the World Sidecar Champions for the 20th *consecutive* year.

The motor cycle world is very competitive just at the moment, with big Japanese multi-cylinder machines vying with Italian exotica of particular splendour; but present quality and past history will always make sure that there are enough enthusiasts to prove that the well-tried Boxermotor and Shaft Drive take a lot of beating.

The beginning of series production at the Aeroplane works on the edge of Munich airfield in 1923. The motor cycle works was marked off from the aero engines by a kind of fence just visible in the background. Horizontally opposed (Boxermotor) engines were used as the firm already had experience of them. The version used in the first motor cycle seen here was developed by Max Friz. This design has remained with the company and although it has obviously been changed in every respect over the years, the basic idea is the same and must have seemed quite wonderfully modern when it was first shown in 1923.

The first production motor cycle, the R.32 (500 cc Side Valve) 1923/6.

The R.37 (500 cc O.H.V.) 1925/6.

The R.39 – first of the vertical engines. 250 cc. O.H.V, 1925/7

Also the R.39 — a contemporary catalogue illustration.

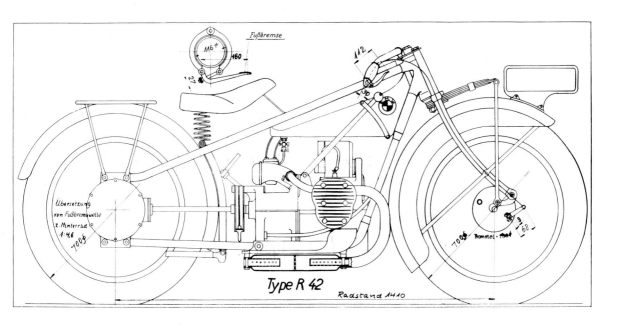

Type R 42

Two illustrations which give some idea of the technical layout of the R.42 the second of the side valve designs — very similar to the previous model, this was in production from 1926 to 1928.

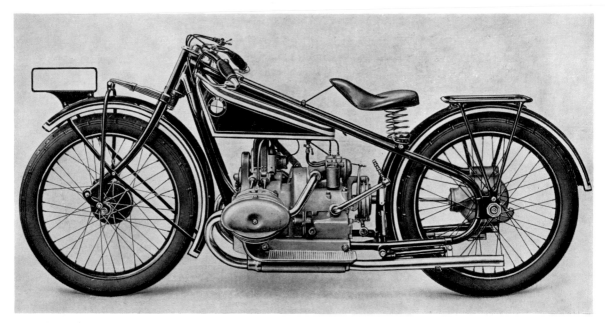

R.57 *looking distinctly sporting* (500 cc O.H.V.) *1927/8.*

R.62 *the first 750 cc (side valve) 1928/9.*

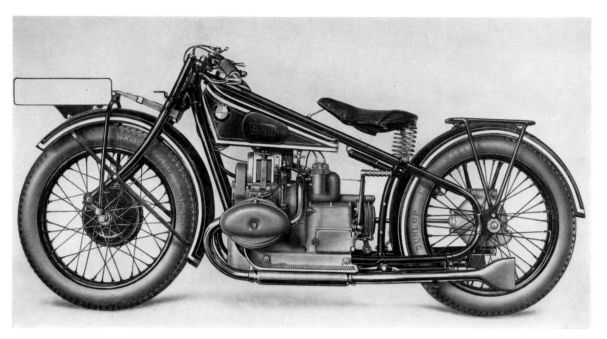

R.57 (500 cc O.H.V.) fitted with the new Sports engine 1928/30.

R.52 (500 cc S.V.) produced in 1928/9 only.

A page of seven-fifties. Above, the 1928/9 R.63 the first O.H.V. 750 cc. Below, first the R.11 Series I (1929/30) a 750 cc side-valve, and then the Series II which was in production 1931/3.

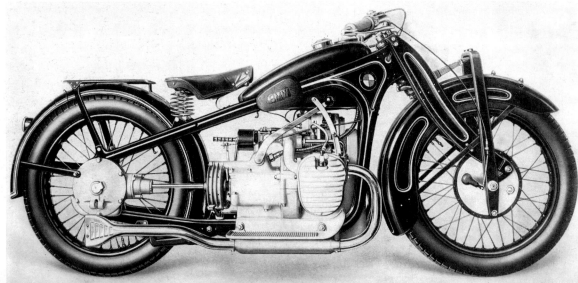

R.16 Series III with two carburettors working directly into the cylinders. Introduced in 1932.

The R.12 in production from 1935 to 1938, a 750 cc S.V. engine was available with either one or two carburettors. This is the single carburettor version.

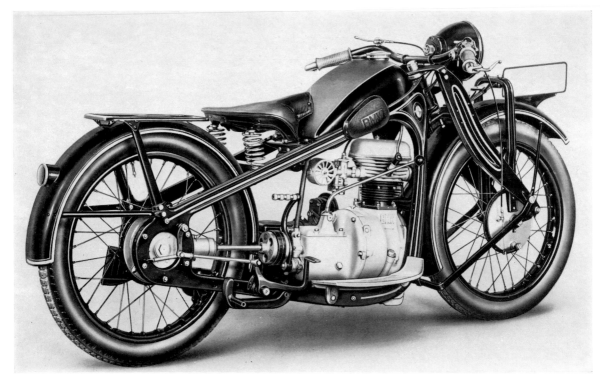

The R.2, a 200 cc O.H.V. single machine in production from 1931 to 1936 with a number of improvements introduced in 1932/4/5 and 36.

The R.4, a 400 cc O.H.V. single which ran a parallel course with the R.2 in time of production and development.

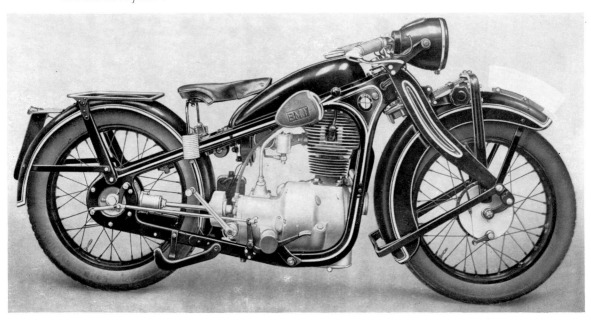

The R.17, a Twin-carburettor 750 cc O.H.V. machine made between 1935 and 1937.

By comparison much more modern the R.5 (500 cc O.H.V.) introduced in 1936.

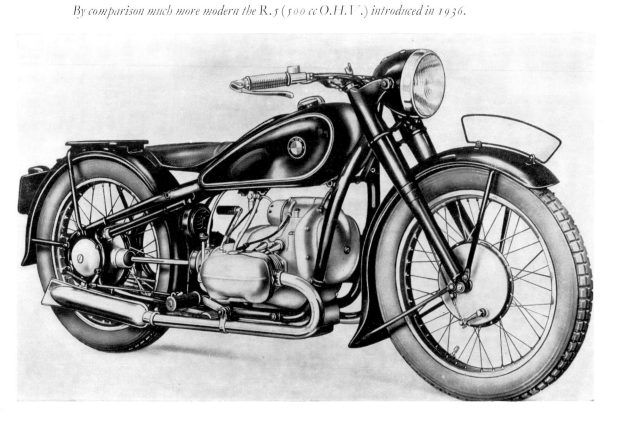

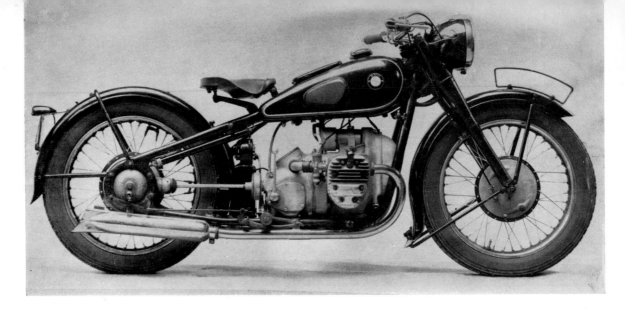

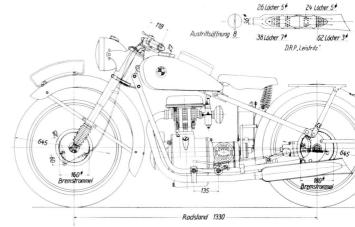

*The immediately pre-war bikes —
a few of which arrived in the U.K.
and caused a major sensation in
motoring as opposed to motor cycling
circles where the "executive" machine
suddenly became a possibility.
Brooklands paddock abounded in
them for a while. Above, the
R.61 and below, backed up by
some technical information, the
R.23 a 250 cc O.H.V.*

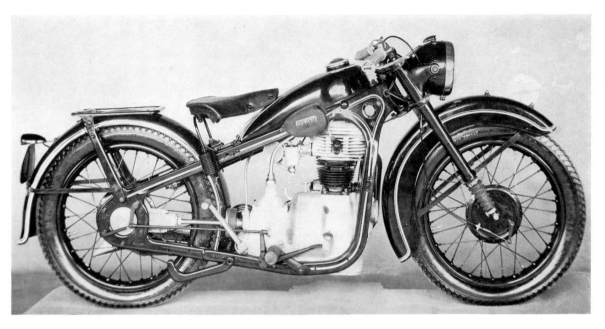

The R.35, a 350 cc O.H.V. made from 1937 to 1939 still using the pressed frame but with telescopic forks.

The last of the pre-war 500s. The R.51 500 cc O.H.V. undoubtedly the apple of the 1939 motor-cyclists eye.

For *those who wanted more power still, the two pre-war 600 cc models. Above, the* R.61
side-valve and below, the R.66 O.H.V.

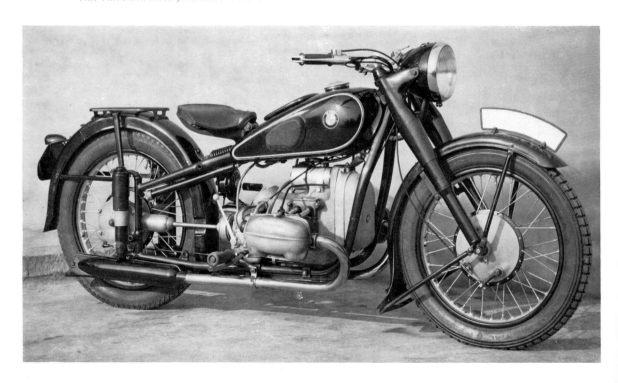

Mostly, one supposes, for side car work, the big R.71 a 750 cc side-valve model much used by the German Army during the war.

As was the special O.H.V. 750 cc R.75 cross country combination seen below.

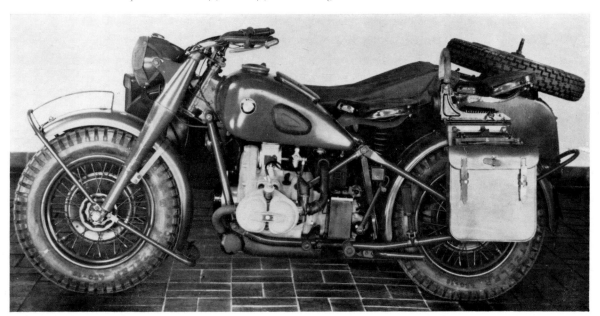

The first post war production permitted by the Control Commission was this R.24 250 cc
O.H.V. model introduced in 1949.

Closely followed by the R.25 of 1950.

These are the two successors to the first post war machine. Above, the R.25/2 of 1951/3 and below, the R.25/3 which was in production from 1953 to 1955. This latter produced some 13 bhp and a very presentable and pleasant performance for a small machine.

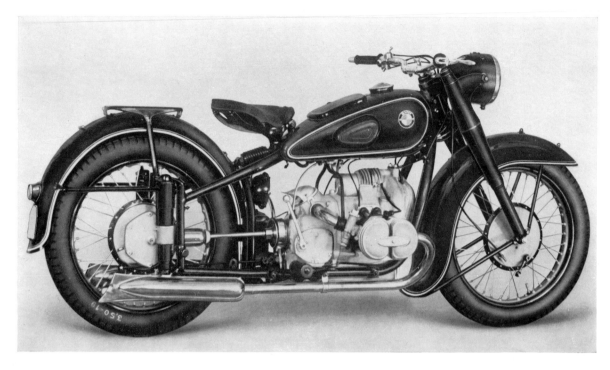

The first of the post war twins. Above, the R.51/2 introduced in 1950 with the 500cc O.H.V. engine and below, the R.51/3 of 1952/3 which was an improved and tidied up version of the same bike.

The R.67 was a 600 cc O.H.V. machine for use either as a solo or with a chair and is seen here in both guises. There were four versions all told running from 1951 until 1956.

The R.68 of 1954, a 600 cc O.H.V. with twin carburettors using a common air-filter.

Almost the last of the 250's the R.26 which appeared in 1955.

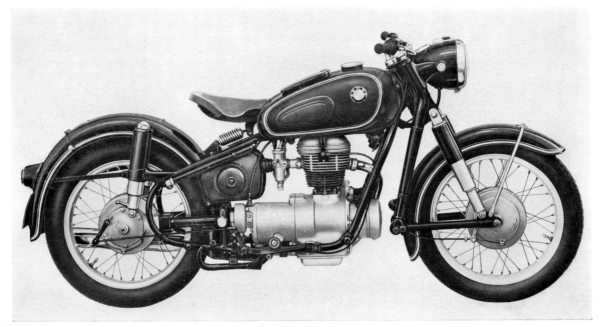

The 1955/6 R.50 and R.60 were indistinguishable.

The R.69 below was in production from 1955 to 1960 and used the 600 cc O.H.V. engine.

The R.50S a 500 cc O.H.V. giving 35 bhp and in production from 1960 to 1963.

The R.69S a 600 cc O.H.V. that was available from 1960 until 1969 — a near ten year run which says something for the stability of the design.

The last of the 250's, the R.27 which appeared in 1960 and ceased production in 1967. 1969 and the R.50/5, R.60/5 and R.75/5 were a like series, as might be guessed of 500 cc, 600 cc and 750 cc rating.

Two views of the R.75/5 the mast-bike of the early seventies and very much the machine that led to the present range.

*Two shots of the 1973 R.60/6.
With a tank holding just over
four gallons, and 40 bhp beneath
it, it had become a formidable
machine. In a world of Japanese
sales success and Italian wizardry,
BMW managed to hold the position
they first achieved in 1923 with a
bike that was in broad principle
the same idea.*

Today's top of the range the R.90S, a 900 cc machine giving no less than 67 bhp and complete to the last detail. A superbike in every respect save perhaps in a recent addiction to garish colours. Henry Ford is supposed to have said that you could have a model T "any colour you like as long as it is black". For nearly fifty years BMW motor cycles went along with that idea. As a last wish let's hope they soon return to it.

George "Schorsch" Meier won the 1937 I.O.M. TT on a blown bike. This was the first time a foreigner on a foreign bike won the race.

Jock West at the top of Bray Hill on a similar machine.

Just before the war this streamlined solo reached 271 kph on the autobahn near Frankfurt. As the run was not made in both directions no official record could be claimed.

Later on a slightly modified machine Ernst Henne managed 279.5 kph

After the war in 1955 Wilhelm Noll with what passes as a side car reached 280 kph on the Munich — Ingolstadt autobahn.

Two racing machines from the early fifties. Above, with the supercharger and below without.

The best known view of a BMW bike racing — their success in the side car classes was, and is absolute — here are Kraus and Huser in 1952.

"Schorsch" Meier in a characteristic pose in 1953.

Enders and Engelhardt in 1969, continuing BMW's unbroken succession of world championships for sidecar machines.

Appendices

Overleaf will be found brief specifications, and in some cases production runs, of the various Eisenach, Dixi and BMW cars and motor cycles.

The ravages of time and two world wars have made some of the early material sparse; but what is available appears here.

Dixi after Ehrhardt, 1904-1928

Some of the principal models, their dates and production runs.

		No. Made	Approx. dates
	Single cylinder, 8 hp	—	1904-06
T.24	4 cylinder, 4.9 litre, chain drive	10	—
T.25	4 cylinder, 4.9 litre, shaft drive	86	—
T.14	2 cylinder, 16 hp	60	—
S.14	4 cylinder, 2.8 litre	110	1904-07
S.15	3.4 litre	75	-10
U 35/3	—	56	-12
T.20	4 cylinder, 4.3 litre, 40 hp	77	1910-13
R.9	4 cylinder, 1900 cc	175	1911-13
T.12	4 cylinder, 2.5 litre, 30 hp	553	1910-20
S.16	4 cylinder, 3.3 litre, 39 hp	710	1913-24
U.1.	4 cylinder, 5.1 litre	78	—
B.1.	1320 cc, 5/14 ps	—	1914
6/24	1600 cc	—	1925
13/60	6 cylinder, produced in small numbers	—	1927
9/40	6 cylinder, identical to Cyklon 9/40 ps	—	1928

Dixi & BMW production of the Austin 7 derivatives

Year	1927	1927	1928/29	1929/31	1931/32
Model	Austin*	Dixi DA1	Dixi DA1	BMW DA2, DA3	BMW DA4
Chassis	—	—	136	268	45
Van	10	—	19	435	—
4 seater Tourer	80	42	4,873	1,834	175
2 seater Tourer	5	—	1,727	1,387	475
Saloon	5	—	1,879	6,600	2,575
Sports Coupé	—	—	674	—	210
Wartburg Sports	—	—	—	150	—
4 door Cabriolet	—	—	—	300	—
2 door Cabriolet	—	—	—	1,374	—
Cabriolet top Saloon	—	—	—	120	—
Production Totals	100	42	9,308	12,468	3,480

*100 complete vehicles were delivered from England.

BMW Production Car Specifications

Year	Type	Cubic Capacity	No. of Cylinders	Bore Stroke	BHP/RPM	Wheelbase in mm	Track in mm	Tyre Size	No. Made
1933-34	303	1175	6	56/80	30/3500	2400	1153/1220	5.25 x 16	2300
1934-36	309	845	4	58/80	22/3650	2400	1153/1220	5.25 x 16	6000
1935-36	315	1490	6	58/94	34/4250	2400	1153/1270	5.25 x 16	10007
1935-36	315/1	1490	6	58/94	40/4500	2400	1153/1220	5.25 x 16	
1935-37	319	1911	6	65/96	45/4200	2400	1153/1270	5.25 x 16	6646
1935-37	319/1	1911	6	65/96	55/4600	2400	1153/1220	5.25 x 16	
1937-38	320	1971	6	66/96	45/4200	2750	1160/1300	5.50 x 16	4185
1938-41	321	1971	6	66/96	45/4200	2750	1300/1300	5.50 x 16	3692
1937-40	325	1971	6	66/96	50/4400	—	—	—	3225
1936	326	1971	6	66/96	50/4400	2884	1306/1400	5.50 x 16	15936
1936-41	326	1971	6	66/96	50/3650 4200	2884	1306/1400	5.50 x 16	
1937-38	327	1971	6	66/96	55/3600	2750	1306/1400	5.50 x 16	1304
1938-40	327	1971	6	66/96	55/4000	2750	1306/1400	5.50 x 16	
1937-40	327/28	1971	6	66/96	80/4600	2750	1306/1400	5.50 x 16	569
1937-40	328	1971	6	66/96	80/4700 4500	2750	1306/1400	5.50 x 16	462
1936-37	329	1971	6	66/96	45/4200	2400	1153/1220	5.50 x 16	1179
1939-41	335	3485	6	82/110	90/3400	2984	1306/1404	6.00 x 16	410
1952-54	501	1971	6	66/96	65/4400	2835	1343/1430	5.50 x 16	2296
1954-55	501A	1971	6	66/96	72/4400	2835	1343/1430	5.50 x 16	1855
1955	501 B	1971	6	66/96	72/4400	2835	1343/1430	5.50 x 16	1267
1955-58	(501) 2.1	2077	6	68/96	72/4500	2835	1322/1408	5.50 x 16	3457
1954-55	502	2580	8	74/75	95/4800	2835	1330/1416	4.5K x 15	330
1955-56	2.6	2580	8	74/75	95/4800	2835	1330/1416	4.5K x 15	5135

Year	Type	Cubic Capacity	No. of Cylinders	Bore/Stroke	BHP/RPM	Wheelbase in mm	Track in mm	Tyre Size	No. Made
1955-63	2.6 L	2580	8	74/75	100/4800	2835	1330/1416	4·5K x 15	2197
1955-63	3·2	3168	8	82/75	120/140 4800	2835	1330/1416	4·5K x 15	2995
1955-60	503	3168	8	82/75	140/4800	2835	1400/1420	6·00 x 16	477
1955-69	507	3168	8	82/75	150/	2480	1445/1425	4·5E x 16	253
1955-62	Isetta	245/300	1	68/68	12/5800	1475	1195/520	4·80 x 10	—
1957-59	600	582	2	74/68	19·5/4500	1700	1220/1160	5·20 x 10	—
1957-63	2600	2580	8	74/75	110/4800	2480	1330/1416	4·5K x 15	431
1957-63	2600 L	2580	8	74/75	110/4900	2480	1330/1416	4·5K x 15	829
1957-63	3200 L	3168	8	82/75	140/5400	2480	1330/1416	4·5K x 15	915
1957-63	3200 S	3168	8	82/75	140/5600	2480	1330/1416	4·5K x 15	834
1959-64	700	697	2	78/73	30/4800	2120	1270/1200	3·50 x 12	—
1961-63	700 CS & LS	697	2	78/73	32/5000	2120	1270/1200	3·50 x 12	—
1961-65	700 Cabrio	697	2	78/73	—	2120	1270/1200	3·50 x 12	—
1962-65	3200 S (Bertone)	3168	8	82/75	160/5600	2480	1330/1416	7·00 x 15	602
1964-65	700 C Long	697	2	78/73	40/5700	2120	1270/1200	3·50 x 12	—
1962-64	1500	1499	4	82/71	80/5700	2550	1320/1374	6·00 x 14	23557
1964	1500	1499	4	82/71	90/5700	2550	1320/1374	6·00 x 14	250
1966-70	1600	1573	4	84/71	83/5500	2550	1320/1366	6·00 x 14	9728
1963-68	1800	1773	4	84/80	90/5250	2550	1320/1366	6·00 x 14	92833
1963-66	1800 Ti	1773	4	84/80	110/5800	2550	1330/1376	6·00 x 14	17850
1968-71	1800	1773	4	84/80	102/5800	2550	1330/1376	6·00 x 14	28852
1964-68	1800 Ti, SA	1773	4	84/80	130/6100	2550	1320/1376	165 x 14	3490
1966-68	2000 Lim	1990	4	89/80	100/5500	2550	1340/1386	165 x 14	51324
1966-68	2000	1990	4	89/80	100/5500	2550	1340/1386	165 x 14	1922
1966-68	2000 A	1990	4	89/80	100/5500	2550	1340/1386	165 x 14	6419
1966-68	2000 Ti	1990	4	89/80	120/5500	2550	1330/1376	175 x 14	6482
1966-68	2000 Ti Lux	1990	4	89/80	120/5500	2550	1330/1376	175 x 14	12080

Year	Type	Cubic Capacity	No. of Cylinders	Bore Stroke	BHP/RPM	Wheelbase in mm	Track in mm	Tyre Size	No. Made
1966-68	2000 C	1990	4	89/80	100/5500	2550	1330/1376	175 × 14	9999
1965-69	2000 CA	1990	4	89/80	100/5500	2550	1330/1376	175 × 14	3500
1965-69	2000 CS	1990	4	89/80	120/5500	2550	1330/1376	175 × 14	9999
1968-75	2002	1990	4	89/80	100/5500	2503	1360/1360	165 × 13	—
1971-75	2002 Ti	1990	4	89/80	130/5800	2503	1360/1360	165 × 13	—
1974	2002 Turbo	1990	4	89/80	190/5800	2503	1372/1372	165 × 13	—
1973-74	2002 Cabrio	1990	4	89/80	100/5500	2503	1360/1360	165 × 13	—
1971-73	2000 Touring	1990	4	89/80	100/5500	2503	1360/1360	165 × 13	—
1968	2500	2494	6	86/72	150/6000	2692	1480/1480	175 × 14	—
1968-70	2800	2788	6	86/80	170/6000	2692	1480/1486	175 × 14	—
1968-70	2800 CS	2788	6	86/80	170/6000	2630	1420/1486	185 × 14	—
1970-75	1602	1573	4	84/71	85/5700	2503	1347/1347	165 × 13	—
1969-74	3.0 S	2985	6	89/80	180/6000	2692	1480/1486	195/70 × 14	—
1970	3.0 Si	2985	6	89/80	195/5500	2692	1480/1486	195/70 × 14	—
1970-75	3.0 CS	2985	6	89/80	180/6000	2630	1420/1486	195/70 × 14	—
1974	3.0 L	2985	6	89/80	180/6000	2792	1480/1486	195/70 × 14	—
1974	3.3 Li	3210	6	89/80	200/5000	2792	1480/1486	195/70 × 14	—
1973	518	1766	4	89/71	90/5800	2636	1406/1442	175 × 14	—
1972	520	1990	4	89/80	115/5600	2636	1406/1442	175 × 14	—
1972	520 i	1990	4	89/80	125/5700	2636	1406/1442	175 × 14	—
1973	525	2494	6	86/72	145/6000	2636	1406/1442	175 × 14	—
1973	528	2788	6	86/80	165/5800	2636	1420/1460	195/70 × 14	—
1975	1502	1573	4	84/71	75/5800	2500	1330/1330	165 × 13	—
1975	316	1573	4	84/71	90/6000	2563	1364/1377	165 × 13	—
1975	318	1766	4	89/71	98/5800	2563	1364/1377	165 × 13	—
1975	320	1990	4	89/80	109/5800	2563	1364/1377	165 × 13	—
1975	320 i	1990	4	89/80	125/5700	2563	1386/1399	185/70 × 13	—

BMW Motor Cycle Specifications

Year	Type	Cubic Capacity	Bore Stroke	HP/ RPM	No. of Cylinders	Tyre Size	Weight in kg	Max. Speed Km/H	No. Made
1923-26	R32	486 cc	68/68	8.5/3300	2	26 x 3	122	90	3100
1925-26	R37	494 cc	68/68	16/4000	2	26 x 3	134	115	175
1925-27	R39	245 cc	68/68	6.5/4000	1	27 x 3.5	110	100	1000
1926-28	R42	494 cc	68/68	12/3400	2	26 x 3.5	126	95	6900
1927-28	R47	494 cc	68/68	18/4000	2	26 x 3.5	130	110	1700
1928-29	R52	486 cc	63/78	12/3400	2	26 x 3.5	152	100	9000
1928-30	R57	492 cc	68/68	18/4000	2	26 x 3.5	150	115	1000
1928-29	R62	745 cc	78/78	18/3400	2	26 x 3.5	155	115	4000
1928-29	R63	732 cc	83/68	24/4000	2	26 x 3.5	152	115-120	1000
1929-34	R11	740 cc	78/78	18/3400	2	26 x 3.5	162	100	8300
1929-34	R16	730 cc	83/68	25/4000	2	26 x 3.5	165	120	1900
1931-36	R2	198 cc	63/64	6/4000	1	25 x 3	108	85	15300
1932-36	R4	398 cc	78/84	12/4200	1	26 x 3.5	137	100	15200
1935-38	R12	745 cc	78/78	18/3400	2	3.5 x 19	162	110	36000
1935-37	R17	730 cc	83/68	33/4500	2	3.5 x 19	165	140	450
1936	R3	305 cc	68/84	11/4200	1	26 x 3.5	149	100	750

Year	Type	Cubic Capacity	Bore Stroke	HP/RPM	No. of Cylinders	Tyre Size	Weight in kg	Max. Speed Km/H	No. Made
1936-37	R5	494 cc	68/68	24/5800	2	26 x 3·5	165	135-140	2600
1937	R6	600 cc	70/78	18/4800	2	26 x 3·5	175	110-115	1850
1937	R35	340 cc	72/84	14/4500	1	3·50 x 19	155	100	15400
1937-38	R20	190 cc	60/68	8/5400	1	3·00 x 19	130	95	5000
1938	R23	247 cc	68/68	10/5400	1	3·00 x 19	135	95-100	8000
1938-39	R51	494 cc	68/68	24/5800	2	3·50 x 19	182	135-140	13000
1938	R61	600 cc	70/78	18/4800	2	3·50 x 19	184	110-115	4300
1938	R66	597 cc	69·8/78	30/5700	2	3·50 x 19	187	140-145	2000
1938	R71	746 cc	78/78	22/4900	2	3·50 x 19	187	120-125	3500
1941	R75	745 cc	78/78	26/4000	2	4·50 x 16	420	95	16500
1949	R24	247 cc	68/68	12/5600	1	3·00 x 19	130	95	12010
1950-51	R25	245 cc	68/68	12/5600	1	3·25 x 19	140	95	23405
1950	R51/2	494 cc	68/68	24/5800	2	3·50 x 19	185	135	5050
1951-54	R51/3	490 cc	68/68	24/5800	2	3·50 x 19	190	135	18425
1951-53	R25/2	245 cc	68/68	12/5800	1	3·25 x 19	142	95-105	38651
1951	R67	590 cc	72/73	26/5500	2	3·50 x 19	192	135	1470
1952-54	R67/2	590 cc	72/73	28/5600	2	3·50 x 19	192	140	4260
1952-54	R68	590 cc	72/73	35/7000	2	3·50 x 19	193	150-160	1453

Year	Type	Cubic Capacity	Bore Stroke	HP/ RPM	No. of Cylinders	Tyre Size	Weight in kg	Max. Speed Km/H	No. Made
1953-55	R25/3	245 cc	68/68	13/5800	1	3·25 × 19	150	108-119	47700
1955-56	R67/3	590 cc	72/73	28/5600	2	F3·50 × 19 R4·00 × 18	192‡ 320†	130†	780
1955-69	R50	490 cc	68/68	26/5800	2	3·50×18	198	130-140	32532
1955-60	R69	590 cc	72/73	35/6800	2	3·50×18	202	150-165	2819
1955-60	R26	245 cc	68/68	15/6400	1	3·25 × 18	158	118-128	30238
1956-69	R60	590 cc	72/73	28/5600	2	3·50×18	195	135-145	20828
1960-67	R27	245 cc	68/68	18/7400	1	3·25 × 18	162	120-130	15364
1960-69	R69S	590 cc	72/73	42/7000	2	3·50×18	202	160-175	11417
1960-63	R50S	490 cc	68/68	35/7650	2	3·50×18	198	145-160	1634
1969-73	R50/5	498 cc	67/70·6	32/6400	2	F3·25 × 19 R4·00 × 18	187	145-157	8650*
1969-73	R60/5	599 cc	73·5/70·6	40/6400	2	F3·25 × 19 R4·00 × 18	192	155-167	21648*
1969-73	R75/5	745 cc	82/70·6	50/6200	2	F3·25 × 19 R4·00 × 18	192	165-175	34397*
1974	R60/6	599 cc	73·5/70·6	40/6400	2	F3·25 × 19 R4·00 × 18	210	155-167	—
1974	R75/6	745 cc	82/70·6	50/6200	2	F3·25 × 19 R4·00 × 18	210	165-177	—
1974	R90/6	898 cc	90/70·6	60/6500	2	F3·25 × 19 R4·00 × 18	210	178-188	—
1974	R90S	898 cc	90/70·6	67/7000	2	F3·25 × 19 R4·00 × 18	215	195-200	—

†With sidecar *As at 30.6.73